LAUGHING
WITH
Lucy

My Life with America's Leading Lady of Comedy

MADELYN PUGH DAVIS
WITH BOB CARROLL JR.

For further information, contact the publisher at:

Emmis Books | 1700 Madison Road | Cincinnati, OH 45206
www.emmisbooks.com

Library of Congress Cataloging-in-Publication Data

Davis, Madelyn Pugh.

Laughing with Lucy: my life with America's leading lady of comedy / by Madelyn Pugh Davis with Bob Carroll Jr.

p. cm.

Includes index.

ISBN-13: 978-1-57860-247-6

ISBN-10: 1-57860-247-5

1. Davis, Madelyn Pugh. 2. Television writers–United States–Biography. 3. Ball, Lucille, 1911- I. Carroll, Bob, 1918- II. Title.

PN1992.4.D315A3 2005

812'.54–dc22

2005013405

Cover designed by Andrea Kupper
Interior designed by Donna Collingwood

Images and dialogue from the *Mothers-In-Law* television series used with permission of Desilu, too, LLC.
Images and dialogue from the *Here's Lucy* television series used with permission of Lucille Ball Productions, Inc.
Alice © Warner Bros, Inc., All Rights Reserved
It's A Great Life photo provided by: Meadowlane Enterprises, Inc.
The Merv Griffin Show photo - Courtesy of Merv Griffin Entertainment
Use of family photos and all other photos not included above - Courtesy of Madelyn Pugh Davis.

Page 154 - The Emmy statuette is the copyrighted property of the Academy of Television Arts & Sciences and the National Academy of Television Arts & Sciences (ATAS/NATAS). ATAS/NATAS also own trademarks for the Emmy name and the Emmy statuette.

Page 255 - *Golden Globe(s)* ®, *Hollywood Foreign Press Association* ® and *Golden Globe* ® statuette design mark are the registered trademarks and service marks and the *Golden Globe* ® statuette the copyrighted property of the Hollywood Foreign Press Association. Copyright © MM-MMV Hollywood Foreign Press Association. All Rights Reserved.

Excerpts from *A Martian Wouldn't Say That* - Courtesy of Leonard Stern and Diane Robison.
Excerpts from *Wake Me When It's Funny* - Courtesy of Garry Marshall and Lori Marshall

Photo prints supplied from the collections of:
Desilu, too, Tom Watson, Michael Q. Martin, Madelyn Pugh Davis and Bob Carroll, Jr.

Photographers:
Front Cover - photo by Tommy Wadelton
Page 46 - Madelyn and Bob Tiny Office - photo by Gabor Rona
Page 180 - Madelyn and Bob Taffy Pull - photo by Ernest E. Reshovsky
Page 217 - Madelyn and Richard L.A. Reception - photo by Lewis & Rhodes Photography
Page 231 - Family returns to Westwood - photo by Ernest E. Reshovsky
Page 258 - Museum of Broadcasting - photo by Jerry Kean
Page 259 - *The Merv Griffin Show* - photo by Saint Amant
Page 265 - Family Group Shot - photo by Michael Q. Martin

We would like to thank all of the photographers who were on staff at the networks and studios and whose names were often not stamped on the backs of their pictures. Photographer Buddy Graybill was on the set of *I Love Lucy* 95% of the time, for the run of the show, and we would like to thank him for his wonderful pictures.

In an age when pictures can be created digitally and sent around the world in a second via the internet, we would hope that people would realize that at some point, a man or woman used their artistry and technical knowledge to create the images that you are enjoying today.

To my husband Richard Davis
with love

Many thanks

to the people who helped me with *Laughing with Lucy*: Lucie Arnaz, Desi Arnaz, Jr, and Elisabeth Edwards at Desilu, too, Sam Semon, Jennika Ingram, Lorra-Lee Bartlett and Peter Murray at CBS, Larry McCallister, Jessica Kaveh, Allan Fogderude, Henry De La Rosa, at Paramount Pictures, Julie Heath at Warner Bros., Bill Allen and Jayne Meadows at Meadowlane Enterprises, Merv Griffin and Robert Pritchard at Merv Griffin Entertainment, Dixon Dern and the Academy of Television Arts and Sciences, Michael Russell and the Hollywood Foreign Press Association, Russell Adams at Schulman Photo Lab, Jeff Ikemiya at JLI Photo Imaging, June Clark at The Peter Rubin Literary Agency, Jack Heffron, Donna Collingwood and Andrea Kupper at Emmis Books, John McLean and Grace Rainer at The Writers Guild of America, Leonard Stern, Diane Robison, Garry Marshall, Lori Marshall, and Stuart Shostak. Special thanks to Laura Levine, Tom Watson, Christina Carroll, and my son Ned Davis.

And a very special thanks to my son, Michael Quinn Martin, and his wife, Donna Coleman Martin, for all their work and help on the book.

Table of Contents

ONE

Don't You Have a Better Joke than That?

NOT LONG AGO, I WAS INVITED TO A LUNCHEON, held in the ballroom of the Beverly Hills Hotel, for women who were TV comedy writers and producers. I was thrilled to see such a large crowd because when I was starting out in television in 1951, you could have held that meeting in a booth at McDonald's. One of these young women said I should write a book because I was a pioneer. This isn't a term I particularly want to put down on my resume, but I went home and thought about it while I churned some butter and made a few quilts. Maybe since I was one of the original writers on *I Love Lucy*, I was some sort of pioneer. Actually, early television *was* a little like going through the Donner Pass in a covered wagon in the middle of winter. There were no maps because nobody had ever been there before, and if you froze to death, or didn't write a funny script, they might draw lots and eat you.

Frankly, I don't know if there can possibly be anything left to say about *I Love Lucy* or Lucille Ball. Lucy has been lionized and analyzed and I, who idolized her, know more about her than I do my own sisters. Well, I will try to offer a few crumbs from a girl-writer point of view. "Girl-writer" is honestly what they called me. This was because comedy shows for people like Bob Hope and Jack Benny were usually written by groups of men who were known as "The Boys," as in "Get The Boys to fix that joke." If they were referring to my partner Bob Carroll Jr. and me, they called us "The Kids," or in Desi's case, "The Kits."

I should warn you before I start that you won't learn any juicy gossip from me because I think it's tacky to write that sort of thing about people after they have died and can't deny it. If you had written unsavory stuff about Lucy when she was still around, she would have come over to your house and hit you with her purse. Authors like to say "the public has a right to know." No it doesn't. And anyway, Bob and I were always the last to hear gossip because we were off in our little office writing dialogue like:

RICKY

Fred, I've got an awful problem on my hands.

FRED

You should have thought of that before you married her.

I remember exactly where I was when I first met Lucy. It's like remembering where you were when they landed a man on the moon. She was the star of a CBS half-hour radio program called *My Favorite Husband.* Richard Denning played her husband, Gale Gordon was his boss, and Bea Benadaret played the boss's wife. We were assembled with the director and the cast around a table in Studio B at CBS at Sunset and Gower in Hollywood. Lucy appeared. She was wearing a pale blue suit and her hair was an amazing shade of red. It was not the more becoming golden-red of later years, but the orange-red usually reserved for sunsets and Raggedy Ann. I later learned she was a frustrated hairdresser, and apparently the henna got out of hand. Now, I had come to Hollywood from Indiana not too long before, and she was the very first real celebrity I had ever met besides Hoagy Carmichael, the Hoosier composer of "Star Dust," and everyone in Indiana had met Hoagy or claimed they had. Bob and I had written lots of radio scripts as staff writers at CBS for the Pacific Network, but this was the first full network script we had ever written. We rehearsed all day and did the show in front of a studio audience in the late afternoon. The two of us sat upstairs in the glassed-in clients' booth during the show, and I hate to admit it, but we counted the laughs—ninety-two. This was it! We were writing a network show for Lucille Ball, and we got ninety-two laughs. We were on our way to The Big Time. Well, not quite.

At that time, *My Favorite Husband* was what was known as a "sustaining" show. That is, it didn't have a sponsor. The network would put a program on and then if it became popular with the audience, an advertising agency would pick it up, and it would be sold to a commercial sponsor. So we were sustaining and things were kind of loose. Bob and I started on the show with the fifth episode and were hired week to week, and often when we came to work in the morning, there would be a writer sitting in the outer office with a script envelope under his arm, and we knew he was there in hopes of replacing us. Also, the network had the right to cancel the show at any time. It was becoming the *Titanic* of sitcoms when Harry Ackerman, the vice president in charge of programming for CBS, hired Jess Oppenheimer to come in as producer/head writer, what they call today a "show runner." Jess had good credits in radio, writing, and

Bob Carroll Jr., Madelyn Pugh, Jess Oppenheimer, and Lucille Ball confer about My Favorite Husband *radio show.*

producing for Jack Benny, Edgar Bergen, and *Baby Snooks* with Fanny Brice. He took charge, and the three of us began writing the scripts together, and things started looking up. It was show twelve when we hit the iceberg.

We were reading the week's script around the table, and at about page six, it became obvious that Miss Ball was less than pleased. She started reading in a monotone, and the room got very still. We finished the interminable script and there was a deadly pause. Lucy got up and stalked from the room and Jess followed her. My life didn't flash before my eyes, but my career did, and it was about to be over before it started. After a while—a year or two—Lucy came back into the room. We read the script again, and nothing was said about her earlier attitude.

We did a large rewrite and later in rehearsal, Lucy linked arms with me and took me over to one side. "I'm sorry," she said, "I've been a big shit." This was 1948 and I had led a

Madelyn Pugh and Lucille Ball discuss a script for My Favorite Husband *radio show.*

rather unsophisticated life in the Midwest, so I mumbled, "No, no, you haven't been what you just said," and Lucy went back to rehearsal. Jess told us later that he had talked to her. She said she didn't like certain things in the script, and he explained that was her prerogative, but that she should understand we were doing the best we could, and if she didn't like some of the jokes or the dialogue, we would fix it.

"A Beautiful Clown"

He told her it wasn't a good idea to treat writers this way, that Bob and I were devastated, and she owed us an apology.

Some weeks later, we heard Desi was out of town with his band, so we invited Lucy to have dinner with us at a great old restaurant in Hollywood called Don the Beachcomber's. We wanted to get to know her, learning her background and foibles so we could write better for her. She accepted, but told us over egg rolls and Mai Tais that she almost didn't come because someone had advised her not to get too close to her writers. Like she might catch a disease or something.

Every fan and interviewer eventually asks me, "What was Lucy really like?" This is sort of a trick question. Have you got a couple of hours? Well, everyone is complicated, and Lucy was more complicated than most. How many of your friends are willing to smash raw eggs in her blouse or set fire to her own nose? Of course, from a comedy writer's standpoint, she was a dream. She made whatever you wrote look great. She was a perfectionist, and if she had to work with a difficult prop, she always wanted the prop there the first day of rehearsal so she could get used to it and find out if there were any problems. She wanted to rehearse and rehearse and get it right, and the more accustomed she was to the prop, the more fun she could have. If she was going to work with animals, she wanted them there the first day, too, so often we would be reading the script and there would be cheeping and barking and braying going on in the background.

Bob and I once told Lucy that she was a beautiful clown. She didn't want to hear it because it embarrassed her, but it was true. She might be dressed in a baggy suit and a battered top hat and wearing big, funny shoes, but she was still beautiful. And unlike some actresses who worry that they won't look good, or their hair will be mussed, Lucy would get into any kind of crazy costume we could think of. She couldn't wait to black out her teeth or get soaking wet or put on a funny wig.

She would often find funny things to do while she was in rehearsal that none of us had foreseen. This is why she insisted on a full-out rehearsal at all times. Actors who were more casual and sort of winged it drove her wild, and since she wasn't exactly known for her tact, she let them know it. She was often blunt and had trouble expressing herself. Or as she put it after biting my head off for something and later sending me flowers of apology, "Why is it that Desi says something and everything's fine. I say something and people get mad?"

She was right, of course. Desi, with his innate charm, would tell you what a great script you had written, "You've done it again, kits!" and say there were just a few little "thins" he wanted changed. And you would gladly rewrite the whole script. Lucy would say, "This script doesn't work at all" when she meant one scene needed fixing, or would ask crossly, "Don't you have a better joke than that?" We felt like telling her we had written a much funnier joke but had sold it to Sid Caesar.

And eloquent she wasn't. Once when she was a guest on the Merv Griffin talk show, Merv asked her, "Do you believe in God?" She thought for a moment and then said, "Well, when you see a sunset or a little baby and stuff like that, if God didn't do it, who the hell did?"

Lucy was loyal. If you look at the credits on all the different shows she did, you will see a lot of the same names. Her hair stylist, Irma Kusely, met Lucy at MGM. Irma was doing Katharine Hepburn's hair, and the first movie she did for both actresses was *Without Love.* She did Lucy's hair from that time all through the various Lucy shows and movies for over fifty years, until 1989 when Lucy canceled an appointment with Irma because she had to go to the hospital. Lucie Arnaz recently told me something that happened at the hospital. They brought her mother back from the operating room after an eight-hour procedure to replace a portion of the aorta. She said the family was all gathered and trying not to burst into tears, and they let them into the hospital room where, she says, her mother was hooked up to every machine that was ever invented. She said she asked the nurse if it would be all right to speak to her mother and if she could talk. The nurse told her yes, but to carefully lift up the oxygen mask and put her head close so she could hear her. Lucie says she bent down, gently lifted the oxygen mask, and she could tell from her mother's eyes that she recognized her, and then Lucy said, "Wouldn't you know this was the day I was supposed to get my hair color done."

Hal King was Lucy's makeup man on *I Love Lucy* in 1951 until she made *Mame* in 1974. Hazel Pierce was her stand-in for at least thirty years. Wanda Clark Stamotovich was her secretary for twenty-seven years, and Frank Gorey her driver for thirty-three.

Bob and I worked with her for a total of twenty years. I think we were like her security blanket. She didn't want us ever to fly on the same plane, and for some reason she wanted us to get married. We went to Europe together once, and when we came home, she asked, "Well, did you get married?" When we said no, she responded huffily, "Well, don't do me any favors!" Interviewers often asked her what she thought was the secret of her popularity and the amazing longevity of her shows, and she always said the same thing: "My writers." Now who wouldn't stick around for that?

TWO

But I Wanted to be a Foreign Correspondent

WHEN I WAS BORN, THERE WERE ALREADY TWO GIRLS in the family and I have a sneaking suspicion my father was hoping for a boy. This feeling was reinforced by the name my parents had picked out for me, which was Isaac after my father and grandfather. My older sister was good enough to share with me that when I came into the world, I had black hair sticking straight out, and since both my sisters were blonde when they were born, my mother saw me and cried out that they had given her the wrong baby. It was hard to figure how this could happen since I was born at home. So here I was, a little girl named Isaac with a bad hairdo. It is small wonder that I became a comedy writer.

I planned to be some kind of a writer at an early age. Not for television because that hadn't been invented yet, but I wrote a play at the age of ten. I was also the director and apparently the producer because I gave myself the title role, talked my friend Jean Miller into being in it, supplied the costumes, and printed the little program, which I still have.

FRENCHY'S WEAKNESS

ACT I "In the Night"
ACT II "The Ransom"
ACT III "The Lost is Found"

CAST OF CHARACTERS
Frenchy
Butch
Betty Brownley
Patricia Ware

There was only one performance and the theater was the living room of our house on Central Avenue in Indianapolis, Indiana. The audience consisted of two people, my mother and my older sister Rosalind. We made up the plot as we went along, and I haven't any idea what Frenchy's weakness was, but I think he was a crook. Apparently, Jean and I played dual roles. All I remember is that I was dressed in a cap and my father's trousers, which were way too big for me. In the middle of the show, I started losing my trousers and quickly ad-libbed "I'll be right back!" and rushed offstage to pull up my pants. My mother and sister were hysterical with laughter at my serious little drama, but I didn't care. I was an author.

I later wrote poetry (no threat to Emily Dickinson), but some of my poems were printed in the monthly paper at Elementary School #84. I learned if you wrote your book reports in verse, you could get an A, even if you hadn't finished the book. We had wonderful teachers who encouraged us to write and put on shows, and one of my efforts was a takeoff on a radio program called *Clara, Lou, and Em*, which I wrote and performed with two of my eighth-grade pals, Harriet Rutledge and Betty Walsh. Another school chum of mine, Reid Chapman, who later became a radio personality in Indianapolis and Ft. Wayne, did a sketch where he played the part of Ben Bernie, a popular band leader at that time, whose signature line was "Yowsah, yowsah," whatever that meant.

It was about then that my mother bought me a second-hand portable typewriter. She was not exactly a stage mother, but you might call her a strong encourager. "Make something of yourself," she used to tell me. She never said what, but I don't think that something was a housewife. She was one of the world's first feminists without knowing what that was. She taught school before she was married and played ferocious tennis, becoming Tri-State Women's champion.

My father was a charming man with a fine sense of humor who told great stories. He was a snappy dresser, wearing spats in the winter and a flower in his buttonhole in the summer. His father died when he was fifteen, and he had to quit school and go to work to support his mother and two sisters. Eventually, he became head of the real estate department of the Security Trust Bank in Indianapolis. He seemed to know everybody in town and whistled everywhere he went.

Many years later, Bob Carroll and I created a TV series that we called *David's Harem.* It starred Tom Ewell, the Broadway actor, and was about a man who had a household that consisted of his wife, three daughters, his sister, his mother, and a female dog, which was the story of my father's life.

In the comics at that time, there was a one-panel cartoon drawn by J.R. Williams that often featured a little guy in a huge cap, known in his family as "The Worry Wort." For some reason, my family used to think this described me as I guess I worried a lot about things when I was a kid. I would write poems to my father on his birthday and sign them "W.W." This characteristic of worrying about everything turned out to be a handy quality when I became a producer.

Madelyn Pugh at 3 years old. "Not called Isaac, but still a bad hairdo."

I think I was around twelve when my best friend and I were talking to her mother about what we would like to be when we grew up. I announced I was going to have a career and be a writer. She expressed a little skepticism, saying, "But don't you want to be married?" and I said, "Yes, I do." "Well,

Lucille Ball and Vivian Vance look through Viv's High School yearbook in The Lucy Show. *Madelyn went to Shortridge High in Indianapolis, Indiana.*

which one is it going to be?" she asked, because in those long-ago days, most men wanted the little woman to stay home and not be doing God Knows What in some office or store. I remember my answer very well. I announced, "I'm going to do both."

I attended Shortridge High School, an excellent school with a great deal of emphasis on writing. There were fine teachers who spent their time encouraging us. There was a yearbook called *The Annual* and a newspaper, *The Echo*, one of the first high-school dailies in the country. I eventually became editor of Friday's edition. Two of my best pals were Ed Ziegner, who was editor of Wednesday's edition, and Howdy Wilcox, editor of Monday's. Ed had a distinguished career as columnist and political editor of the *Indianapolis Star-News*. Howdy also wrote for the *Star-News*, was a major-general in World War II, and founded his own public relations firm. Characters with Ed and Howdy's names eventually found their way into some *Lucy* scripts. There were some noted authors who graduated from Shortridge: Louise Wilde O'Flaherty, who has written nine Gothic novels; Beurt SerVaas, who became CEO of the Curtis Publishing Co.; Dan Wakefield, who at last count had written fifteen fiction and nonfiction books and several screenplays; and Kurt Vonnegut, who became Kurt Vonnegut.

I was vice president of my senior class (the president was always a boy, right?). The worst thing you could do was cut class and hang around the drugstore across the street and smoke. I know it sounds like an old MGM Judy Garland-Mickey Rooney movie, and it was a little like that. We danced the Jitterbug and went crazy over Indiana basketball. We "double-dated," and hung out at a drive-in called "The North Pole" on Saturday night. First your date got his father's car. Then you went to the movies, and afterwards you drove round and round "The Pole" to see who else was there, usually the people you had just sat next to at the movies.

Lucy went to Vivian's high-school reunion in an episode on *The Lucy Show* and we called Viv's high school "Shortridge," and the principal Joel Hadley, the name of my real principal. When she first read the script, Lucy wanted to change the name of the school to Jamestown, her alma mater. I didn't say anything, but Bob spoke up and said, "That's Madelyn's high school," so she left it alone.

Meanwhile, in St. Petersburg, Florida, Bob Carroll was editor of his high-school yearbook: the *No-So-We-Ea*. Bob thinks it must have referred to the fact that people came from North, South, West, and East to the city, a tourist attraction. Bob remembers going to dinner parties in junior high. He thinks it was to teach all the kids table manners, but he remembers it as a good way to meet girls. He said he used to ask his father for some funny things to say at the party since his father had been an amateur entertainer and had a stock of old jokes. We borrowed some of these when we wrote "The Benefit" episode of *I Love Lucy.* Lucy has talked Ricky into being in a show with her at Ethel's club. They plan to do an old-fashioned vaudeville number where they wear striped suits and straw hats and carry canes. They sang "We'll Build a Bungalow" and stopped for jokes in between the lyrics:

RICKY

A tramp came up to me on the street and said he hadn't had a bite in days.

LUCY

What did you do?

RICKY

I bit him.

In rehearsal, Lucy finds out that Ricky has taken all the jokes for himself and given her the straight lines, so when they performed the bit for Ethel's club, it went like this:

RICKY

A tramp came up to me on the street and said he hadn't had a bite in days.

LUCY

What did you do, bite him?

This episode also contained one of our biggest laughs.

Before Lucy got Ricky to do the song-and-dance bit, she is trying to talk Ethel into wearing a horse costume with her, where Ethel is the back end of the horse. She assures Ethel that no one will recognize her. Fred comes in the door, looks over at the hind end, and says, "Hi, Ethel."

Long before I was writing rear-end-of-horse jokes, I attended Indiana University in Bloomington, Indiana, and majored in journalism. I was a reporter on *The Daily Student*, the campus paper. I never aspired to be editor-in-chief because it was almost always a man and anyway it was a lot of work, and I was having a pretty nice social life. I joined Kappa Kappa Gamma sorority, which gave me sixty instant friends. This was good because I was seventeen years old when I went to college and hadn't ever been away from home before, unless you count two weeks at Camp Kosciusko on Lake Tippecanoe. (Would I make up names like that?)

The summer before my senior year, I went on a trip with four of my sorority sisters to Los Angeles. We borrowed Marge Little's mother's car (Marge later married Charlie Van Tassel, and their names crept into various *Lucy* scripts), took turns driving, and stayed in motels. Betty Jo Hanson, one of the passengers whose name also appeared in a script, reminded me recently that we each had one hundred dollars, and it had to last us four weeks. One of those motels was situated right next to the train track, and in the middle of the night a train came roaring by, and the whole room shook. When the Ricardos and Mertzes took their trip to Hollywood, they stayed in a similar motel and had the same experience, maybe just a teensy bit exaggerated.

When *I Love Lucy* first went on the air, our sponsor was Philip Morris Cigarettes. That was in the bad old days before people knew about the dangers of smoking. Their commercials used to boast about how Philip Morris had a "secret ingredient" (and we all know now what that was). We were requested not to use the word "lucky" in a script because one of their big competitors was Lucky Strike, so we would say someone was "fortunate." It took me years to get over feeling guilty when I said "lucky." So let's just say I had a pretty fortunate childhood. One of the less fortunate things was that my father lost all his money in the Depression of the 1930s. He had invested heavily in real estate and, of course, you couldn't even give it away. Banks were foreclosing on peoples' homes, not to mention closing the bank entirely. It was very hard on him, and he spent the rest of his life repaying his debts because he didn't think it was the honorable thing to declare bankruptcy. So money was a little tight in our house.

In a way, this was probably also fortunate for me because I learned to scrounge around, trying to get summer jobs and scholarships for my tuition. I ran a store at the Kappa house where I bought cigarettes and candy wholesale and sold them retail. I started up a late-night snack business in my room (grilled cheese sandwiches and Cokes). This was back in the dark ages when women college students had curfews, and everyone always got hungry after hours when they were studying. But I opened one night and was closed down the next because somebody pointed out that cooking in the rooms was against the fire laws. Maybe it was just as well because for several weeks, my clothes reeked of melted cheddar.

My senior year, the Japanese bombed Pearl Harbor, and the country was suddenly at war, so I decided what I really wanted to be was a foreign correspondent. My heroes were William Shirer, who covered Germany and later wrote the book *Berlin Diary*, Howard K. Smith, who wrote *Last Train From Berlin*, and Ernie Pyle, Indiana's favorite son, who traveled with the army and wrote a column about the ordinary GIs at the front. I didn't buy myself a trench coat, and I kept my ambitions to myself.

Lucy and Ricky do a vaudeville act and use Bob's father's old jokes.

Somebody pointed out that there were very few women foreign correspondents, but there were very few women anything, so it didn't bother me.

I graduated and began looking for a job. I had taken shorthand my last year in college in the Business School at IU without credit because I thought if all else failed, I could get a job as a secretary and work my way up into becoming some kind of writer. I was vaguely aware that you don't start out being a foreign correspondent right away, and it might be a good idea to see if I could become a reporter on a newspaper first. Incredible as it seems now, the only job a woman could get at most papers at that time was on what was known as "The Society Page." This was an account of weddings, parties, and general social news.

There were three papers in my home town: *The Indianapolis Times*, *The Indianapolis Star*, and *The Indianapolis News*. Each paper had a staff for the society page consisting of a woman editor and one woman reporter. But I wasn't proud. My plan was to get on the society page and then pull off some great scoop ("Groom Elopes With Bridesmaid?") and impress my bosses so they would have to make me a real news reporter. I had an interview with each of the papers, and they were too kind to point out that there were no jobs for people without any experience. I got the feeling that to get on the society page staff, the editor had to die, and then her assistant would be promoted and some lucky (excuse me, fortunate) lady would get hired. I also had interviews for writing advertising copy, having taken two whole courses in advertising in college. I graduated in June, and two months later I was still unemployed. I went to Chicago to visit my older sister Audrey and tried my luck there, but Chicago didn't want me, either. I was seriously considering joining the Women's Army Corps.

To be perfectly honest, I did have one job offer as the editor of the in-house newspaper of Kingan's meat-packing plant. Kingan's was a reputable plant, but on summer nights on the south side of Indianapolis, there would be a strange, unpleasant odor wafting about from the stock yards. We would look at each other, nod, and say "Kingan's." I turned the job down because I didn't want to spend my life extolling the virtues of rump roast. Anyway, someone with the last name of Pugh really shouldn't write for Kingan's.

I am fascinated by the way serendipity or fate or chance or whatever you want to call it plays a part in our lives. At this point, Dick Davis, a med student I had been dating in college who knew I was still out of work, suggested that maybe I should go see Jane Allison, a friend of his brother Joseph. Jane was working at WIRE, the local NBC radio station. I didn't like to

Madelyn Pugh at Indiana University with her portable typewriter.

ask, "What do they write there?" I shared the views of most radio listeners that they just made up that stuff as they went along. But I was not in a position to be picky, so I went to see Jane at WIRE on top of the old Claypool Hotel in downtown Indianapolis. The Claypool (now the Embassy Suites) was built in 1903 and was often the sight of political conventions.

The lobby was full of marble pillars, potted palms, and big brass spittoons, and there was a plaque on the side of the hotel that said Abraham Lincoln had made a speech on that corner on his way to Washington to be inaugurated. (No, no, not while I was working there.) WIRE was owned by Eugene Pulliam, who also owned a lot of newspapers, and neither of us knew that his grandson would turn out to be former Vice President Dan Quayle. I had an interview with Jane Allison, who must have sensed my desperation, because she offered me a job at twenty dollars a week.

I might as well admit right now that I wouldn't have had any career at all if it weren't for World War II. Jane explained that there was an opening on the writing staff because the man who held the position joined the Navy. Later, I was hired as a staff writer at CBS Hollywood because some man got drafted.

I found out that "what they write" at radio stations is a little bit of everything, including commercials and patter for disc jockeys. "And now for a change of musical pace, a platter by Tommy Dorsey and his orchestra as they ask the musical question, 'Who?' " Jane was the head of the department and I was the staff. A week after I started at WIRE, *The Indianapolis Times* offered me a job as a reporter. I was in a quandary. This was the job I really wanted. But it didn't seem right to quit a job after a week, and they HAD asked me first. So I turned it down and gave up that trench coat forever.

When I look back, I realize I had my own agenda and must have been what we used to call "a pain in the prat." After I had worked at WIRE for awhile, I asked for more money. "I've been here six months, and I'd like a raise," I announced. They gave it to me, and I was now making twenty-five dollars a week.

My sister Rosalind, who had been singing with a band, married the band leader and moved to Los Angeles with her baby daughter Sharon. My father had died my last year in college, and my other sister, Audrey, was in Chicago; so my mother thought it would be a good idea to get some of the family together. She loved California, having visited there when Audrey trained show horses at a stable (now the site of the Bel-Air Hotel). In those days, a bridle path went down the median of Sunset Boulevard, and you took the Red Car if you wanted to go way out to Santa Monica to the beach. I think my mother tried to get my father to move to California. He would probably have made a fortune in real estate there, but he had a good job, and his family lived in Indianapolis so it didn't happen.

We made the decision to move to Hollywood. After all, I had experience in broadcasting. I had worked at WIRE a whole year. Becky Endres, my friend from college, decided to go with us.

We sold the family Oldsmobile to get money for the trip, which sounded like a feasible idea. Who needs a car in Los Angeles, right? I quit my job at WIRE, and they not only gave me a goodbye party, but Mr. Pulliam gave me letters of introduction to CBS, ABC, and NBC. I was appreciative but not overwhelmed. I mean, didn't everybody get letters of introduction to the West Coast executive vice presidents of all three networks?

My mother made an arrangement to drive a car out for a dealer and deliver it to San Diego, and off we went on Route 66 in a used De Soto convertible. No one was making new cars because of the war. The three of us sat in the front seat (no bucket seats yet) with our small dog riding on the deck behind us. Becky and I took turns driving. We read the Burma Shave signs, which would later be used in the *I Love Lucy* episode "California, Here We Come." Meanwhile, Bob had made three round trips from Florida to California with his mother, father, and three sisters in a seven-passenger

Bob Carroll Jr. at five years old looking debonair with his saxophone.

Packard, so he remembered the "Aunt Sally's Pecan Pralines" signs for that show. You know, "Five miles to Aunt Sally's Pralines," "One mile to Aunt Sally's Pecan Pralines," "500 yards to Aunt Sally's Pecan Pralines," and then when they finally got there, a sign on the door that said Aunt Sally was out of business.

The De Soto convertible was perfectly fine but the tires weren't, which no one had bothered to mention. On the trip out, we had four flats. We developed a system. The tire would blow, and we would pull over to the side of the road. Becky and I would get out, unload the trunk to get out the spare, and then look helpless. It usually only took a few minutes before some gallant man stopped and changed the tire. (Remember when men were gallant and how handy that was?) We both knew how to change a tire, but there was no use in getting all dirty if we didn't have to. Sexist? You bet. Then we would drive to the nearest town and my mother would go to the ration board to stand in line and apply for a retread tire so we could have a spare for the next time this happened. You had to have a good reason for traveling in war time and getting a decent tire, so my mother told them Becky and I had jobs at an aircraft plant in Los Angeles, which we might have if we didn't find the jobs we wanted. Then we would unload the trunk again, put in the spare, repack the trunk, and get back on the road. It took us nine days to drive 2,000 miles, but we finally arrived in Los Angeles, where we got lost on the Pasadena Freeway but eventually found my sister's apartment.

The next day, I went to the NBC Radio Network and presented my letter. I was given an appointment with Executive Vice President Sid Strotz, who hired me as a staff writer. My outfit for the interview was a little hat, gloves, high heels, and a dress made by my sister. Becky got a job as a secretary with Ruthrauff and Ryan, an advertising agency, just down Vine Street from NBC. This turned out to be fortuitous because she ended up marrying Bill Burch, an account executive for R&R, who later produced *The Tennessee Ernie Ford Show.* Meanwhile, Bob Carroll was working in the mail room at

CBS Radio, a block away on Sunset Boulevard.

We stayed at the William Penn Hotel on Alvarado Street, and Becky and I went to work from there. The staff at NBC was very small—Caryl Coleman, the boss, Harriet Reagh, Evelyn McCutcheon, and me, all in one tiny office. About this time, I sold a poem to the "Postscripts" page of the *Saturday Evening Post* magazine, and for about a week I was the biggest celebrity in the room.

My mother found a small house for rent around the corner from my sister, and we settled in. The rent was seventy-five dollars a month, which a government office later reduced to fifty dollars a month (we never asked them to) because you weren't allowed to charge exorbitant rents just because there was a war on.

I remember writing my first program at NBC, a musical show of some sort, that was to be aired at 7:30 A.M. I set my alarm and got up to listen. A totally different show came on. I panicked. Didn't they like my script? Did I file it at the wrong time? Would I get fired? And other good questions. Well, it turned out I hadn't done anything wrong. NBC didn't own the local outlet KFI, who put on their own program, and my clever lines went winging out to Yakima, Washington, or Provo, Utah, or whatever Pacific Network outlet didn't have anything better to broadcast.

On weekends, Harriet Reagh and I wrote a revue made up of music and satirical sketches about radio. It was called *It's in the Air*, and it opened and closed the same night. One reviewer said, "Last night I saw *It's in the Air* and my advice is to stay upwind."

THREE

Worse than Married

After six months of doing flop musicals and writing for Yakima, I decided it was time to move on, so I walked down the street and talked CBS into hiring me. They owned their own 50,000-watt radio station, KNX, and had a large staff of writers. You could even hear your own work if you tuned in. Kathleen Hite was the first woman writer hired and I was the second. See how the war and the shortage of men keeps cropping up here? I mean, no one actually wanted to hire women in 1944, but what else was there? I believe there was some theory going around that women were just filling in until all the men came home from the war and then things would go back like they used to be. Surprise!

Besides there not being enough men, there apparently weren't enough offices at KNX, so for two weeks I worked in the supply closet that I shared with another young writer,

E. Jack Neuman, who had been hired the same day. We had one typewriter between us, and part of the ceiling was slanted so we kept bumping our heads. I later learned that Bob Carroll and another writer, Larry Roman, shared the closet when they first started on staff. Maybe it was some kind of basic training to teach you stamina and how to walk about bent over.

I have never understood why executives and producers get great big offices (sometimes with kitchens and butlers) but writers, who have to slave away in their offices all day, get little crummy ones? Well, I know why it is, but I don't want to talk about it. Neil Simon swears that when he and his brother, Danny, worked on the TV show *Caesar's Hour,* their office was the landing on a staircase. Later, when Bob and I were writing *I Love Lucy* at General Services Studios, we had such a small, dark office, we had to keep the lights on all day. We finally got two miners' caps with little lamps on the front from the prop department, turned out the overhead lights, and kept working with the door open. It wasn't long before we collected a chortling crowd and pretty soon we had a bigger office with two windows and our first real honest-to-goodness secretary named Denni Massey.

But even though I was working in a closet, I felt being at CBS was progress. Bob, too, had moved along in his career and was no longer in the mail room, but had graduated to staff writer. Soon, I was writing a half-hour radio drama every week called *Romance of the Ranchos* about stories that happened in the early days of California, and Bob was writing for a show called *Pot Luck Party,* starring Jack Bailey, who went on to become the emcee of *Queen for a Day*.

The staff set-up at CBS was a great place for young people to break into the business. Some who got their start there were Blake Edwards, the movie director; John Michael Hayes, who went on to write *Rear Window* and *To Catch a*

Thief for Alfred Hitchcock; Kathleen Hite, who later wrote hundreds of TV scripts for *Gunsmoke, The Waltons,* and *Falcon Crest*; Larry Roman, who wrote *Under the Yum Yum Tree* and *Alone Together* for Broadway; and E. Jack Neuman, my closet buddy, who later created *Mr. Novak* and *Dr. Kildare,* and became a TV and movie producer.

Don Thornburgh, executive vice president of CBS West Coast, was a wonderful man and a mentor for the writers. He used to follow our careers and took great pride in our accomplishments. Most of us started at low-level jobs at the network. Larry Roman was a "door boy" for *Lux Radio Theater*, which often had big stars recreating their roles from movies. His job was to run errands and keep unauthorized people away from the stage. Bob Carroll began on the information desk in the lobby and then graduated to the mail room; Kathleen Hite was a secretary, and E. Jack and I were junior writers. One of Mr. Thornburgh's biggest successes was Ernie Martin, who started out as an usher, and later formed a partnership with Cy Feuer and produced *Guys & Dolls, Where's Charley?, How to Succeed in Business Without Really Trying,* and other big Broadway musicals. Mr. Thornburgh was originally from Indianapolis, and one day he stuck his head in my office, asking, "Where's the little girl from Indiana?" Instead of doing my weekly script assignment, I was writing a personal letter to a certain captain overseas and almost threw my body over my typewriter. The staff was a great training ground. I learned to grind out scripts every week, and if I didn't have an idea, I'd better get one fast. I stayed there for four years.

About the third year, John Dunkel and Tommy Tomlinson, who headed the staff, put Bob and me together as a team to write a half-hour show called *The Couple Next Door* about some newlyweds. We wrote twenty shows a season, so when we would "pull an all-nighter," we would get sick of our little tiny office sometime around midnight and Leo, the night cleaning man who became one of our best buddies, would let us into Mr. Thornburgh's office and we would work there. His office was on the top floor, was very large, and had big windows on two sides. I am appalled, even now, to think of what gall we had to work in the chief executive's office without his permission. I am glad he wasn't driving by and looked up to see paper airplanes flying out the windows of his office. When we got stuck on a joke, we used to fly planes out the window to see which one went the farthest down Sunset Boulevard.

Next we were assigned to a half-hour Pacific Network show called *It's a Great Life* for a new young comic, Steve Allen. This consisted of three sketches, with the popular singer Kay Starr doing a song in between. A typical sketch was one about how Jack and the Beanstalk would be handled if it happened today and the media reported it. Chet Huntley, a young newscaster at CBS West Coast (who later became half of the Huntley-Brinkley NBC news team), was a guest, and he did an on-the-spot report which went like this:

CHET

This is Chet Huntley, down at the bottom of the stalk. Jack has just arrived with the goose who lays the golden eggs, and we're going over to see if we can't have a word with him. The police have cordoned off the area and—here comes the giant now, climbing down the stalk after Jack!

SOUND: CRASHING FOOTSTEPS

CHET (CONT'D)

Mr. Giant, I wonder if I could have a word with you.

GIANT

Fee-Fie-Fo-Fum! (GROWLS)

Steve Allen confers with Producer/Director Milt Stark and writers Bob Carroll Jr. and Madelyn Pugh for the It's A Great Life *radio show.*

CHET

Well, that's very interesting, Mr. Giant. Tell me, how do you feel – no, no, Mr. Giant, put me down! (STRUGGLING) Wait! No! Back to you at the studioooooooooo!

HIS VOICE TRAILS OFF.

People often ask me what it's like to write as a team. Jerry Lawrence, a playwright, was a friend of mine and he and his partner Robert E. Lee were the authors of *Inherit the Wind, Auntie Mame,* and other Broadway hits. Jerry always wanted us to do a play about being a man-woman writing team and call it *Worse Than Married.* We never got around to doing it, but Jerry wasn't far from wrong. Being a part of a writing team is a little like being married, only you get to go home at night to somebody else. But let's face it, you are together a lot! Fortunately, neither Bob nor I liked arguing. Our idea of having a big fight over a line was to say something sarcastic, have a four-minute snit, and then get on with the script. Bob

Schiller and Bob Weiskopf, who later worked with us on *I Love Lucy*, had an argument over a joke one time, and Bob Weiskopf left the room. After an interval, Schiller asked their secretary, "Where's Weis?" She answered that he got in his car and went home.

About the only thing Bob and I really fought about was the temperature of the office. Apparently, we have totally different body thermostats. On more than one occasion, we would be walking down the street to lunch and I would wear a sweater and jacket, and he would be in shirt sleeves and shorts. One time, the temperature in our office was so uncomfortable and chilly (to me) that I brought a small baby blanket and wrapped it around my legs, but that didn't solve the problem because when people would see me, they thought I was ill, like a little shut-in who ought to be wheeled out in the yard to get some fresh air. Roz Moore, TV writer-producer, has told me when she was a show runner for *Home Improvement*, one of the big problems working with mostly a male staff was that they kept the room at a freezing temperature. So maybe it's a guy thing.

I do know that one of the man-woman differences was the attitude about hair. It used to get on male nerves how often I had mine done. I went every three weeks for cut and color to my hairdresser, Mr. Billy. Unfortunately, I couldn't go early before work because he worked in a salon at the old I. Magnin store, and they didn't open until ten, so I used to take a long lunch break. Bob was fairly patient about this, but it seemed to nettle Schiller and Weiskopf. Later, when they wrote *Maude*, they had Bea Arthur's character go to a hairdresser named "Mr. Billy." Lucy's hairdresser, Irma Kusely, solved my problems by offering to do my hair on the lot, which saved a lot of time, so they stopped complaining.

Fortunately, Bob and I have the same sense of humor. Once when we were having a reading for a special we were doing, we both wrote the same word to be added to a joke to make it better. Actually, writing with a partner is rather comforting psychologically. If he doesn't have an idea for a story, maybe you will. And if you can't come up with a good joke, maybe he will. He is also someone who can pick you up when you have to have your car repaired. You bounce lines off each other. Maybe one of you suggests something and, while it isn't exactly right, it can make your partner think of something else that is better. We used to laugh a lot when we were writing. If you're writing by yourself and you laugh a lot, people tend to avoid you.

Another plus to having a partner, if you are having a personal crisis, the other one can take over. During the years we wrote together, we had two weddings each, three divorces (one for me and two for him), one child apiece (Christina Carroll for him and Michael Martin for me), and numerous operations for Bob, some for his hip which had bothered him since he had contracted osteomyelitis as a child, one for a bleeding ulcer, and another for a broken shoulder. On more than one occasion, I took a portable typewriter to his hospital room and we worked out of there. It's not that we were brave or masochistic or anything, but as Bob says, when Lucy sits down at the table to read the script for the first time, there had better be something for those anxious little hands to pick up.

Our way of working was to sit facing each other at two identical desks with two lamps and two typewriters. Then I typed the script (I was the girl and my mother made me take typing in high school, right?), and Bob would pace around the room. This became a problem when we later worked at my house because when Bob would act out some of the comedy business, my neurotic poodle would rush over and fiercely grab Bob's pants leg. Either he didn't like Bob jumping around or he thought the routine wasn't funny. We would

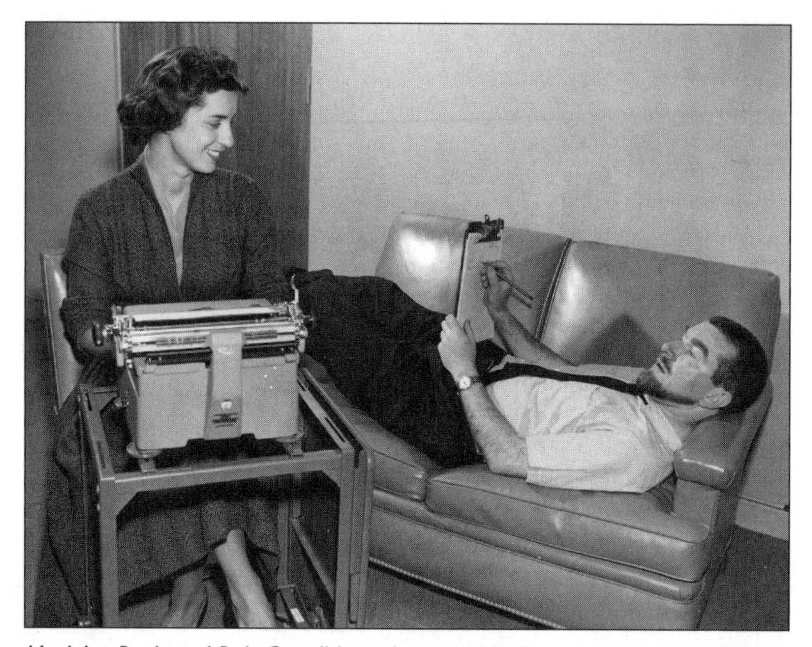

Madelyn Pugh and Bob Carroll Jr. in their tiny My Favorite Husband *office.*

write a few lines, I would read them back to him so we could hear how they sounded, and then we would write the next line. I typed the script on two sheets of paper with a carbon in between. This was back in B.C.—Before Computers. Also before Xerox, so when I finished a page, I would give Bob the carbon copy. Bob claims it was years before he found out that all scripts weren't slightly blurred.

One day, Bob and I went to lunch to discuss how we could get on a "network" show, that is, big-time radio, coast to coast. We made a list of shows we'd like to work on and put CBS's *My Favorite Husband* starring Lucille Ball on the top of the list. Some friends of ours, Bill Davenport and Frank Fox, who were the writers on the show, told us they were leaving to go back to work on *Ozzie and Harriet* in the fall. They promised to put in a good word for us, so Bob and I thought we'd try for it, although Bob said he didn't want to get tied down and why didn't we see how it went before we committed to each other as a team. Or as he put it, "I'll give it a year," which was over 50 years, roughly 300 radio shows, 400 TV shows, 250 producer credits, umpteen pilots, and five movies that were never made ago.

We approached Harry Ackerman, then network vice president of programming for CBS West Coast, and asked if we could write a script for *My Favorite Husband.* Harry said yes. We asked will you pay us, and he said no, and we said okay. You can see we were tough negotiators. We wrote a script and, much to our surprise, they bought it. The show was about a young married couple, George Cooper (played by Richard Denning) and his wife Liz (played by Lucy). George volunteers Liz's talents to teach the boss' teenage nephew to samba. The nephew, Wally, didn't learn very fast or, as Liz put it, "Wally dances the samba like a kangaroo with hot coals in its pouch." The problem was, Wally had never held a woman in his arms before and thought he was in love with Liz. To discourage him, she told him that she couldn't leave her husband because he was so old and needed her. Richard Crenna played the teenager and was terribly funny.

We later reworked the script for *I Love Lucy,* calling it "Young Fans." Dick Crenna again played the teenager, and we added a girlfriend of his, Peggy, who was a fan of Ricky's and was played by the actress Janet Waldo. The kids are intrigued by Lucy and Ricky, a "fascinating older couple." To discourage them, the Ricardos, in the TV version, pretend to be really old, dressing up with white hair and glasses. Lucy tells Peggy that Ricky, who is in a wheelchair, has rheumatism, so she should lift his legs up on the coffee table so he'll be more comfortable.

LUCY

And jiggle his legs.

PEGGY

Jiggle them?

LUCY

Yes, you have to keep them moving or his arteries harden.

PEGGY LIFTS RICKY'S LEGS UP ON THE TABLE AND JIGGLES THEM.

PEGGY

I don't understand this. Ricky, your hair—when did it turn white?

RICKY

You've never seen it like this, have you? I don't bother with the shoe black at home. Keep jiggling.

PEGGY JIGGLES RICKY'S LEGS MORE VIGOROUSLY.

PEGGY

Is that better?

RICKY

Yes. You're a much better jiggler than Lucy.

PEGGY

Thanks. I can't believe this whole thing. Why, I just saw you at rehearsal yesterday, dancing around and beating your conga drum.

RICKY

Yes. I'm glad you saw that, Peggy. That was my farewell performance.

LUCY

Yeah. He's Baba-ed his last lu.

Janet says to this day, even though she has played many other parts, including the voice of Judy Jetson on *The Jetsons,*

I Love Lucy *Episode "The Young Fans" with Richard Crenna and Janet Waldo. This was based on a* My Favorite Husband *episode which also featured Richard Crenna.*

when people hear her name, they want her to autograph her picture "Keep jiggling, Peggy."

Harry Ackerman wanted us to start writing for the show immediately. He offered $250 a week for the two of us, so we resigned from our staff jobs. Because we had to quit so abruptly and felt we were leaving Steve Allen in the lurch, we gave him our hundred-dollar fee to write his own show that week. I decided I was so rich, I bought my first car.

After a rocky start, *My Favorite Husband* was sold to a sponsor and was on the air for two-and-a-half seasons. At the end of that time, Ackerman and Don Sharpe, Lucy's agent, thought Lucy would be perfect for the new television medium and decided to do a pilot with her using her radio show as the basis. Lucy wanted Jess, Bob, and me to write her new series, but she didn't want to do *My Favorite Husband,* even though she liked the actor Richard Denning. She wanted to do a show where her husband was played by her real husband, Desi Arnaz. Desi was on the road with his band so much that they seldom saw each other, and this way he could stay home. At one point in their lives, Desi and his band were playing at The Mocambo nightclub on the Sunset Strip, and Lucy was working in a movie at RKO Studios in Hollywood. He got off work around 2 A.M., and she went to the studio for makeup at 4 A.M., so they used to make a date to meet halfway on Mulholland Drive. Then she would go to work, and he would go home to bed.

The network didn't feel the audience would believe Lucy was married to a Cuban band leader. Lucy told them stubbornly that she *was* married to a Cuban band leader, and the audience would like it fine. To prove this, she and Desi decided to get audience reaction by going on the road with a stage act and asked Bob and me to write it. Desi would do his usual show and sing with his band, and Lucy would keep interrupting, trying to get into the act. The material included Desi singing "Cuban Pete" with Lucy making a "surprise" appearance and doing a take-off called "Sally Sweet." This was later incorporated into an *I Love Lucy* episode called "The Diet." Later in the show, Lucy came from the back of the house dressed as a clown, in a baggy suit and floppy hat, carrying a cello, demanding to play with the band. Desi let her "try out," and she did a routine with a trick cello, which was created for her by a friend of theirs, a clown named Pepito. As Desi says in his autobiography, "This whole act eventually became the pilot for *I Love Lucy.*"

The pilot was shot on March 2, 1951, in front of an audience in Studio A at CBS, Columbia Square. It was put on a kinescope, which was a film copy made from the TV tube. There was no three-camera film system because Desi hadn't invented it yet. (Videotape, what's that?) The sets were a nightclub and a living room with walls that were so flimsy, when you closed the door they shook, which was par for the course on live shows at that time. Lucy's wardrobe consisted of a large bathrobe and a baggy clown suit since she was now pregnant with Lucie Arnaz. Pepito did one of his routines in the nightclub scene. The show was produced by Jess Oppenheimer and directed by Ralph Levy, who was also directing *The Burns and Allen Show* TV program, which was done live every two weeks. Jerry Hausner played Ricky's agent. Later, we did the pilot over on film, and it ran as the sixth episode in the series.

Originally, we named the characters Lucy and Larry Lopez, but someone pointed out there was a popular band leader at the time named Vincent Lopez, and it might be confusing. We changed it to Ricardo and changed Larry to Ricky. When I looked at the pilot script recently, I was surprised to see we had written that the show opened with "voice over" narration and showed the exterior of the Ricardos' apartment building in New York City. This was a device left over from radio where an announcer "set the scene." It was pretty "cutesy," and it was all cut when finally filmed, thank goodness.

I have to admit something. In the pilot, Lucy is begging Ricky to let her in his show at the club so she will have a shot at being on television. Ricky's next speech was as follows:

RICKY

I want a wife who is just a wife. All you have to do is clean the house, bring me my slippers when I come home at night, cook for me, and be the mama for my children.

Why she didn't brain him with those slippers, I'll never know. Mea culpa! But it was 1951, and Lucy and I didn't know any better. The redeeming factor is that in the script, Lucy did get into the act, and the network offered her a TV appearance instead of Ricky.

After we did the pilot, Bob was taking off for Europe and I decided to tag along, since I wanted to see Europe but didn't want to travel by myself. We had been gone about four weeks when we went to American Express to pick up our mail and found a cable from our agent Ben Benjamin. (We named the agent Ben Benjamin in "Ricky's Movie Offer" and he was played by the fine comedy actor Frank Nelson.) We were very excited. I immediately wrote to my mother in Los Angeles on May 8, 1951, on some of that tissue-paper-like stationery they used for airmail in those days:

Dear Mother:

We drove to Naples and picked up a cable from Ben Benjamin at American Express, who said the Lucille Ball-Desi Arnaz show was sold for fall. CBS is offering us $800 per show to write it. He advised us to accept, and we did.

Love,

Madelyn

What I didn't tell her was Bob and I were having such a good time that for one giddy moment, we considered pretending we didn't get the cable. A very smart decision that would have been. Apparently, I was running out of money, or as I explained in my next letter:

Dear Mother:

Had a letter from Jess and he said the Lucille Ball-Desi Arnaz show is going to be on the air between Arthur Godfrey's *Talent Scouts* and *The Goldbergs* on Monday nights, which is good. He says he wants to get some scripts written this summer and start filming in September. We should get home about the third of June. Although flying home will cost another $150, I think I'll be okay financially with a job to come back to.

Love,

Madelyn

So we came home and started writing scripts with Jess. Today, a sitcom series usually does twenty-four scripts a season, but the three of us figured we would have to write thirty-nine scripts for the first season like we did in radio. We didn't know any better. We were making things up as we went along.

FOUR

The Cuban Arm

WHEN WE DID THE PILOT OF *I LOVE LUCY,* THE CAST consisted of Lucy, Ricky, Pepito the clown, and Jerry the agent. In those days a show only had one sponsor. We were told that Milton Biow, head of the Biow Advertising Agency, was considering the show for his client Philip Morris Cigarettes, and he ran it for his good friend Oscar Hammerstein II of the famous Broadway team of Rodgers and Hammerstein. "Here's a little comedy we might be sponsoring. What do you think?" Hammerstein said, "It's okay, but you should have neighbors." As it turned out, Oscar was absolutely right. Any man who can write *The Sound of Music* should be listened to. If Lucy plans to save money on her grocery bill by buying a second-hand freezer and getting her meat wholesale, who else is she going to tell but Ethel? And if Ricky is afraid Lucy is a kleptomaniac, who else is he going to confide in but Fred? So, now we had neighbors.

Someone had told Jess that we should have eight scripts before production started, so we began writing. We had a basic idea for a series, and there was no doubt about Lucy's comedy talent, but we didn't know who would play the neighbors, and they weren't even named yet. We didn't know what the sets were going to look like or where the show was going to be shot, and we didn't know if Desi could play comedy. So, we would begin writing a script by saying to each other, "The neighbors, whoever they are, come in the front door, wherever it is, and Ricky is sitting on the couch, if there is one, and says something funny, and we hope he can handle it."

While we were busy writing, a small bomb was dropped. Desi got a call from Milton Biow, who told him he thought they were going to have a great show and casually asked him, "When will you be moving to New York to start your new series?" At that time, almost all the big hit TV shows were done in New York because the largest audience was on the East Coast. There was no coaxial cable, so the rest of the country saw a "kinescope," which was very poor quality. Desi sputtered that they hadn't planned to move to New York. Mr. Biow politely made it clear that they weren't interested in a show that originated on the West Coast, and Desi hung up in shock. His and Lucy's dream of working together and living with their new baby on their little ranch in the San Fernando Valley was about to go up in smoke.

There have been a lot of books written about Lucy, but none about Desi except for his autobiography. The general impression seems to be that he was a lucky Cuban who was handsome, charming, played the bongo, and happened to be married to the funniest lady in the whole world. Well, this was all true, but there was a lot more to Desi than that. He may have only been that when he started, but he had an amazing ability for learning things and he was an astute businessman, even though he only finished high school. He also liked and appreciated writers, which I consider a really fine characteristic in a person. And let's face it. He *was* charming. I don't know where those Latins learn that. Maybe they teach it in the third grade. We all used to joke about the "Cuban Arm." If Desi put his arm around your shoulders and called you "amigo" or "parner," you were cooked. I remember one time he invited Bob and me to have lunch in his private dining room. We were just finishing a season and were very tired, so before we joined him, we made a promise to each other whatever he asked us to write, we were going to say no because we badly needed a vacation.

Two hours later, we came out of his office, having agreed to write a movie and two pilots on our time off. He also was one of the most positive people I have ever met. When somebody told him it was impossible to do something, he would ask, "Why not?" Lucie Arnaz told me recently that her dad's philosophy was "There must be a way."

So Desi thought about his new problem, and he says in his book that someone, somewhere, touched his shoulder and said "film," or maybe in his case it was "el cine." Okay, so you do the show on film, but what about having an audience because Lucy worked best before a live audience? He called CBS and told them what Mr. Biow had said, and that he and Lucy wanted to do the series in California, and how about doing the show on film in front of an audience? They told him he couldn't do that, and he naturally said, "Why not?" And they said, because it's never been done, and he said, "Why not?" I'm not sure who he called "amigo" or "parner," but CBS gave him half-hearted approval to see what he could work out, probably hoping he would come to his senses.

At this point, I'm sure someone is muttering, "Big deal! Everybody does three-camera sitcoms on film or tape in

Lucy and Ricky in the pilot for I Love Lucy.

front of an audience." Ah, but not in 1951. Videotape hadn't arrived, although there were a few TV shows being done on film. *Amos and Andy* was using one film camera and showing it to an audience later and recording the laughs. Ralph Edwards was using three film cameras on *Truth or Consequences,* but the cameras were stationary and there was only one set. Jerry Fairbanks was using three 16mm film cameras on tripods.

Eddie Feldman of the Biow Agency knew a man named Al Simon who had worked with Edwards. He was hired as a consultant and given the title of associate producer. Lucy and Desi got in touch with Karl Freund, director of photography for MGM, and talked him into joining the group. He was an Academy Award-winning cameraman and had no intention of doing TV, but he couldn't resist the challenge of lighting a set so you could use three camera angles all at once. Marc Daniels was hired as director.

In an article in *Cinemeditor*, Dann Cahn, the first film editor of *I Love Lucy*, recalls that Lucy and Karl Freund were from the movies, Desi was an actor and a band leader, Jess and Bob and I came from radio, Al Simon was a writer who was involved in TV-film production, and Marc Daniels was from the New York stage and live television. It was a motley crew, but somehow it all came together.

Most of the shows coming out of New York were done in theaters, so a search was started for an available theater in Los Angeles. None of these seemed right. Al Simon got a call from a friend and went to look at an old movie studio called General Service on Las Palmas Avenue in Hollywood. At first, Al didn't believe a soundstage would work at all, but the more he thought about it, there would be a lot more room for sets, and if they rented the stage for the season, some of the sets could be left standing from week to week. He figured that a door could be made in an outside wall so the audience could come in from the street. He called Desi and Jess and they came over and looked around, and before long they realized they had their theater. They named it "Desilu Playhouse."

There were lots of glitches. Putting the audience in theater seats wouldn't work because everything was on the same level and no one would be able to see over the cameras. Herb Browar, the new stage manager, suggested bleachers, which solved that problem. The floor was full of nail holes from all those years of building sets, so they covered it with masonite so the cameras, mounted on crab dollies, could move smoothly in all directions during filming. The first show was done straight through with only one intermission like a play because we thought the audience would be bored if we stopped for anything but reloading the cameras. When we found out that people were fascinated with the whole process, we changed and took breaks between scenes, and Desi went out and talked to the audience. This gave us a lot more opportunities to use funny costumes and props.

The editing of the show was complicated and very time consuming. Dann Cahn and his assistant Bud Molin were using a moviola to view the film, but they had three complete half-hour pictures to cut together each week, and they were barely making their deadlines. George Fox had an idea which he took to Mark Serrurier Jr. (whose father invented the very first moviola), and he devised a three-headed moviola so you could look at three versions of the show at the same time. Danny and Bud affectionately called this device "The Three-Headed Monster." Quinn Martin was hired as sound editor. Today, the moviola has been mostly replaced by a digital nonlinear computer system. Danny tells me that his father Philip Cahn, and Quinn Martin's father Martin Cohn, who were film editors in the '20s, used to cut film with a magnifying glass and a pair of scissors over a frosted glass light well.

Emily Daniels, Marc Daniels' wife, became the industry's first film camera coordinator. She had been called an assistant director in live TV in New York, but that title and position were already taken in film. She talked to the cameramen and grips on an intercom during the show and told them to move to various marks that had been earlier taped on the floor. One night, an overzealous new cleaning man took up the unsightly tapes, and they all had to be done over the next day.

A major glitch happened when someone discovered that the show would cost a lot more money if we did it on film. CBS balked at the extra expense, and for a moment it looked as if the whole project was off. Don Sharpe, Lucy and Desi's agent, shrewdly suggested that the two take a big cut in pay to make up the difference, and he negotiated that, for taking

Producer Jess Oppenheimer, Lucy, Madelyn Pugh, and Bob Carroll Jr., backstage at I Love Lucy. *The brick wall is the backside of the Ricardo's fireplace.*

a cut, they would own the negatives of the films. CBS agreed. After all, what value were TV shows that people had already seen, right? What do you mean "reruns in syndication?" The head of CBS Business Affairs told Bob and me that everybody had to take a cut in salary to pay for the extra cost and docked us both $25 each show. I like to think that the reason you can still see *I Love Lucy* today is because of our fifty bucks.

Marc Daniels had worked with Vivian Vance in New York, and when he found she was appearing in a play, *The Voice of the Turtle*, in La Jolla, California, he persuaded Jess and Desi to drive down to see her. They liked her a lot and went backstage after the show to talk to her. She wasn't interested in doing television since she was a stage actress and was up for a part in a film at Universal, but they talked her into it. Originally, we all wanted Bea Benadaret and Gale Gordon from *My Favorite Husband* to play the neighbors, but they were both under contract to other shows and weren't available. So they hired Vivian, and it was an inspired choice.

Lucy had worked with Bill Frawley in movies, and when he heard she was doing a series, he called to see if there was a role for him. I understand the part had been offered to Jimmy Gleason, another fine character actor, who turned it down. In those early days, many movie actors considered TV beneath them and thought it was a passing fad and would go away. When one remembers those grainy little black-and-white screens and the fact that people used to stand outside appliance stores and watch the shows through the window, who can blame them?

And we needn't have worried about whether Desi was funny or not. He learned comedy very quickly. In the episode "Job Switching" (the show where Lucy and Ethel worked on a conveyor belt in a candy factory), he and Fred had a scene where Ricky has totally miscalculated how much rice he should make, and the rice boils out of the pot, all over the stove, and onto the kitchen floor. They had never done the scene with real rice until the actual filming and nobody realized how slick rice gets when you step on it. Desi accidentally slipped and fell flat, but acted like it was part of the scene. He then managed to slip "accidentally" to get two more laughs before the scene was over. One of my favorite lines is Fred's answer to Ricky in the first part of the scene:

RICKY

Hey, listen, by the way, what do you know about rice?

FRED

Well, I had it thrown at me on one of the darkest days of my life.

One of our problems was how to handle Desi's accent. Should we ignore it or make fun of it or what? We learned the hard way not to write the accent into the script. We knew that he said "Take a tizzy" for "Take it easy," but if we wrote "Take a tizzy," he would say clearly, "Take it easy." We also learned that the audience resented it if we had anyone else make fun of his English besides Lucy. Apparently, other people making fun of his English was insulting, but she could do it because it was done in a loving manner. Once in a while there was an exception. In the episode "Lucy Goes to Monte Carlo" in the fifth season, Ricky has made Lucy promise not to gamble, and she picks up a chip from the floor, places it on the roulette table and inadvertently wins a lot of money. She doesn't think Ricky will believe her, so she hides the money in the Mertzes' closet. Ricky finds the money and mistakenly thinks Fred, who is acting as his band manager, has juggled the books and stolen the money from him. Fred is outraged.

RICKY

Fred, I'm afraid I've caught you red-handed.

FRED

You have not caught me rett-hanna, you Cuban mushmouth!

In this case, Fred could be insulting because he meant to be insulting. Desi confessed years later that he often didn't understand some of the jokes in the show (the ones that perhaps were based on knowledge of American idioms), but he never let on. He figured if we all thought it was funny, it must be funny.

We filmed the first *I Love Lucy* on September 8, 1951, and it was all very exciting. Because Desi started out as a nightclub performer, he liked to give the audience a real show. His band, under the direction of Wilbur Hatch of CBS, played in between scenes, and the sets were screened from the audience by curtains. Lucy and Desi considered the audience an important part of the show. We never did retakes or pick-up shots until after the audience left. The announcer, Roy Rowan, would introduce Desi and he would come out, welcome everyone and tell a cute, clean joke (if you like, I can come over to your house and tell the joke word for word, complete with accent, because I probably heard it more than two hundred times). He would then introduce the cast, Lucy being last.

In the audience at every show were Lucy's mother, Desi's mother, my mother, and Bob's parents, who always sat in a row. Lucy's mother usually brought along five or six friends. Bob swears his father started "spontaneous" applause after an especially funny bit. When Lucy made her appearance, she would parade up and down in front of the bleachers, and then she would introduce her mother, whose name was Desiree, but everybody called her Dede. Lucy would say, "I want you to meet my beautiful Dede," and her mother would stand up and take a bow.

The first episode filmed was "Lucy Thinks Ricky is Trying to Murder Her" and the first one on the air was "The Girls Go To a Nightclub." I don't remember why they were switched. What I do remember are the reviews after we went on the air October 15, 1951. Most of the reviewers liked Lucy, but were very lukewarm about the writing. *Weekly Variety* called it "one of the slickest entertainment shows to date," but added, "if the story line wasn't exactly inspiring, nevertheless it had a flexibility for a full-blown exposition of Miss Ball's talents." *Daily Variety* said, "The laughs were there and plentiful... but the plotting should be more inventive and less contrived just for the sake of laughs." Dan Jenkins of *The Hollywood Reporter* gave it a rave, saying, "Keep your eyes peeled for this one. It's a honey." *Time Magazine* wasn't exactly bowled over. They said, "*I Love Lucy* is a triumph of bounce over bumbling material. Comedian Lucille Ball romps engagingly through a series of vaudeville routines, gets adequate assistance from her husband Desi Arnaz, and raucous support from veteran actors William Frawley and Vivian Vance."

When I read the *Time* review, I thought it said "bounce over *bubbling* material," and I figured that wasn't so bad, until I read it again.

We would all like to have that certain intuitive capacity for knowing when something will be a success or not. Of course, if you did, you would be hired to run a studio or a network. You can have the most talented actors, the best scripts, and a good time slot, and it bombs anyway. With all the glitches and our collective inexperience, our first show landed in the top ten of the ratings, and it looked as if *I Love Lucy* was a hit. People have speculated about why it has been so tremendously popular. Well, I'm not much on theories. Maybe it was the right show for the right time. Or it could have been Desi's business smarts, or Jess's fine producing ability, or the way the great ensemble cast interacted. Who can say? But Desi once said, and I agree with him, "Ninety percent of the success of the show goes to Lucille Ball and the rest of us can divvy up the remaining ten." Lucy had an incredible gift for farce. In some of the things she did, there were traces of those giants of the silent screen—Chaplin, Laurel and Hardy, and Buster Keaton, who was a friend, and once gave her some tips. One of these she took to heart, which was to always be familiar with your props.

At one of the recent *Lucy* conventions, Bob and I were on a panel answering questions from the audience and someone asked, "When you were writing the first *I Love Lucy* scripts, how did you know Lucy was so physically funny if you had only worked with her in radio?" It was a good question and one that had never been asked of us before. Once we started thinking about it, there were a lot of reasons. First, we had seen her do comedy in the movies. When we were doing

Frank Stanton, President of CBS, Bob Carroll, Jr., Madelyn Pugh, Desi Arnaz, O. Parker McComas, President of Philip Morris, and Karl Freund, I Love Lucy *Cinematographer, celebrate* I Love Lucy *winning the Sylvania Television Award at the Hotel Pierre on December 11, 1952.*

My Favorite Husband, she was also making *Miss Grant Takes Richmond* with William Holden and *Fancy Pants* with Bob Hope. At the time, Lucy told us we wrote such good physical gags, we should write for the movies. She had always had a comedic flair, starting with one of her very first pictures in Hollywood. According to the story, it was a movie called *Roman Scandals* starring Eddie Cantor, and she was a Goldwyn Girl, a beautiful chorus girl without any lines. Eddie needed somebody to get hit with mud when the villain is aiming at Eddie and misses, so Eddie asked which one of the girls wanted to do it. Lucy immediately held up her hand and said, "Me! Me!"

There were other signs of her talent for physical comedy. If she was telling you a story about something that happened to her, she would act out all the various parts. It was wise not to sit next to her or she would use you as a prop. She and Desi were living on their ranch in the San Fernando Valley. They had planned to raise chickens, but when we met her, the chickens were very old, and Lucy had named them and couldn't bear to kill them. As she told the story, she strutted around like an old, old chicken, and gave us a pretty good idea that she could do funny visual things. Much later, we used this in the episode "Lucy Raises Chickens."

There were also the commercials she did with our announcer Bob Lemond at the end of each *My Favorite Husband* episode. We were sponsored by General Foods and the product they were advertising was Jello Pudding. The commercials were based on Mother Goose rhymes. Bob would tell the story, for instance, of Little Miss Muffet who was eating Jello when along came the spider played by Lucy, who used a funny voice and made a certain sound, and so later we wrote SPIDER in the script, which meant she should make a sound like "eeuh!" It became such a trademark that in the episode "The Ricardos Change Apartments," we had Lucy, Fred, and Ethel all do a "eeuh" together. We had certain shorthand we wrote in the script. We used the direction PUDDLES UP when we wanted her to look as if she is about to cry and LIGHTBULB when we wanted her to let the audience know from her face that she has come up with an idea.

In the stage act Bob and I wrote for Lucy and Desi, she was dressed as a clown who plays the cello and wants to be a member of Desi's band. Desi says he'll have to see her credentials. The clown misunderstands what he means by "credentials" and looks shocked, like "how dare you!" and clutches her coat around her, so whenever we wanted her to do that look, we wrote CREDENTIALS. Another direction was something we saw her do in rehearsal, a little tight-fisted gesture of frustration. This was known as a DRATS. Both hands made it a DOUBLE DRATS. In "Lucy Writes a Novel," Ricky, Fred, and Ethel find out that Lucy is using them as characters in an unflattering light. They burn her manuscript, and when she announces she has made a carbon copy, the three each do a DOUBLE DRATS. After a few years, Lucy got a little self-conscious about doing the SPIDER, and in "The Star Upstairs" script, Bob and I wrote in the directions LUCY DOES A SPIDER FOR THE FIRST TIME IN A LONG TIME, and Lucy did a modified "eeuh."

One of the first awards *I Love Lucy* received was the Sylvania Award given by the Sylvania Company, who made TV sets, in the fall of 1952. Desi, Karl Freund, and his wife, Bob, and I, went back to New York for the occasion. Lucy was pregnant with Desi Jr. and didn't think she should travel. The president of Philip Morris, our sponsor, took us to the 21 Club for lunch along with Desi and the president of our advertising agency, and Bob and I felt very important. That night after he accepted the award, Desi took our group to a nightclub called La Vie En Rose, where Nat King Cole was appearing. The maitre d', whose name was Tony, hailed Desi and put an extra table on the dance floor just for us. In between sets, Nat came and sat with us. It was all very grand. Desi went home to be with Lucy, and Bob and I stayed on to see some Broadway shows. One night we thought we'd go to La Vie En Rose again. We went in saying, "Hiya, Tony," to our old pal, and he gave us a tiny table by the kitchen. Apparently, we weren't quite so grand when we weren't with Desi Arnaz.

Later that season, Lucy told a story about being in New York with Desi. They went to the theater to see a musical and when they walked in and started down the aisle, people began to stand up and applaud. She said she whispered to Desi, "Some celebrity must have just come in." It wasn't until they reached their seats that they realized the applause was for them.

On another one of their trips to New York, they appeared on *The Ed Sullivan Show* at a testimonial in their honor. Lucy was introduced, and she named all the people who had contributed to *I Love Lucy* and graciously thanked them. Then Ed Sullivan introduced Desi, who said, "My first job when I came to this country was cleaning bird cages. We came to this country from Cuba, and we didn't have a cent in our pockets. From cleaning canary cages to this night here in New York is a long way. And I don't think there is any other country in the world that would give you that opportunity. I want to say thank you, America, thank you." By now he was very emotional and teary and so was Lucy. Ed Sullivan even unbent from his usual stiff self and gave Desi a sort of half hug.

Desi was truly grateful for the good things that happened to him. His father was the mayor of Santiago, and the family was wealthy. They had to flee Cuba, leaving everything behind, because of the Batista political revolution. He once remarked that he started with nothing and ended up married to a gorgeous woman, had two beautiful children, and a hit TV show. He often said to himself, "Desi, you are a very 'locky' guy."

At the end of that season, at the Emmy Awards banquet at the old Coconut Grove in the Ambassador Hotel, Red Skelton won for best comedy performance. He accepted it by saying, "You've given it to the wrong redhead. I don't deserve this. It should go to Lucille Ball." Then he came to our table and made a mock ceremony of presenting the award to Lucy.

We wrote thirty nine scripts for that first season, filmed them all, and aired thirty five, saving four for the next season. Bob and I kept hoping that the President would preempt us by giving a speech on Monday night so we could get a week ahead because no one did reruns in those days. General Service Studio wasn't open weekends, so we brought along a wooden box to stand on, and climbed over the wall in order to work in our office. We also worked holidays. One New Year's Eve, we wrote until eleven, changed into our party clothes at the studio, and went to Hans and Margaret Conreid's annual New Year's Eve party in time to usher in the New Year. Hans was the wonderful, funny character actor who often appeared on *I Love Lucy.*

One of the shows we saved for the next season was the candy-making episode. Before we filmed it, Jess gave an assignment to Herb Browar to find a "candy dipper" who would not only be in the scene but show Lucy what to do. Herb went to the See's Candy factory and found Amanda Milligan, whose job all day long was to take the little cream fillings, swirl them around in the chocolate sauce, and place them on a tray. He hired her, and she came to rehearsal. Lucy watched her in action and immediately found a funny way of being very bad at the dipping Amanda did so expertly. During a break, Herb asked Amanda how it felt to be on television. She answered, "I've never been so bored in all my life!" Originally, she was supposed to have lines, but she had a problem with them because she wasn't an actress, so the lines were cut. When Lucy tried to make conversation with her in the scene, she totally ignored her and kept on with her job, which made it funnier.

Lately, a story has emerged that we shot the candy-making scenes in See's Candy factory. Well, as much as I am a devoted fan of See's Candy, this simply isn't true. All the scenes were done in front of the audience in the totally fictional Kramer's Kandy Kitchen, cross my heart and hope to die from eating too many butter creams.

Herb told me another behind-the-scenes story about the

Lucy and Ethel make candy in the "Job Switching" episode of I Love Lucy. *The Foreman, played by Elvia Allman, says "Speed it up a little!"*

show. During the candy dipping, Lucy discovers a fly buzzing around, she tries to catch it and when it lights on Amanda's face, she smacks at it with her hand covered with chocolate. Amanda was supposed to slap her back. During rehearsal, Amanda was very tentative about hitting the star, and the bit wasn't working. Herb says he watched in admiration as Lucy was very gentle in the dress rehearsal, but on the show she smacked Amanda hard. He said Amanda did what anybody would do when she gets slapped in the face, she hauled off and let Lucy have it, as Lucy knew she would.

There was also a story in the paper not long ago about Edelweiss, a Beverly Hills candy establishment, and how Bob and I got our inspiration for Lucy making candy from their store. Well, criticizing people who make chocolate is to me like saying things against the flag, but that isn't true, either. The way we came up with the candy idea is much more prosaic. (It's like when I found out that Stephen Sondheim, the Broadway lyricist and composer, used a rhyming dictionary.)

Jess and Bob and I were working out the story line for the script, and we wanted a funny job for Lucy and Ethel to end up doing, so we got out the phone book and looked in the *Yellow Pages*. When we got to "C," we said, "Aha! Candy making!" Then Bob and I went to the Farmer's Market on Fairfax Avenue and watched a woman dipping chocolates to see how she did it.

Having an authentic candy dipper was typical of the way things were done on the show. Lucy liked to have the real thing so she could first learn how to do it right and then could have more fun doing it wrong. The more accustomed she became to the props, the more she could find funny things to do with them and make it look spontaneous. Herb Browar remembers that during the filming of "The Amateur Hour" in the first season, Lucy was working with a rubber frog, and she complained it wasn't lifelike. So he had to go find a frog farm somewhere and bring back a real frog and two stand-in frogs. Also in "Pioneer Women," Lucy was rehearsing with a fake wooden loaf of bread, and she said, "It doesn't feel right." So Herb had the Union Made Bakery make a practice loaf and another one for the TV show when the huge long loaf of bread bulges out of the oven and pins Lucy to the wall. The bakery didn't have a pan big enough, so Herb found a sheet metal shop in Hollywood and had a pan made to order. The baker suggested making the bread out of rye so it would stay fresh longer, and Herb says after the show was over, the crew ate rye bread for days.

The candy-making show was one of my favorites, and we opened the second season with it.

FIVE

Lucy Isn't Pregnant, She's Expecting

WE WERE GETTING READY TO TAKE A VACATION before the second season when Desi came into Jess's office one day, looking worried. "We've just come from the doctor's office," he said, "Lucy's 'spectin'." They were delighted about the baby, of course, but apprehensive about what this would do to the show. Jess said, "That's wonderful! This is just what we need to give us excitement in our second season. Lucy Ricardo will have a baby, too." Desi rushed off to tell Lucy, and Jess later admitted he had some second thoughts, wondering if he spoke too quickly. As quaint as it seems now, no one had ever shown a pregnant woman on TV before. If an actress happened to be pregnant and was needed in a scene, she would be dressed in a big coat or placed behind a chair. CBS and the Biow Agency were not at all enthusiastic. Milton Biow felt that two shows about the pregnancy would be plenty, and CBS thought the whole thing was a disaster. Harry Ackerman of CBS later said that in hindsight it was probably the best thing that ever happened to the show.

Of course, the schedule had to be changed to accommodate Lucy having some time off, so we all shortened our vacations and began filming early. In those days, there was a department at the network called "Continuity Acceptance" and they watched everybody's scripts like hawks to be sure they were squeaky clean. No four-letter words or bodily functions, please. We were told we couldn't say the word "pregnant," but to say Lucy was "expecting" or "enciente." Nowadays, you can not only say "pregnant" on TV, you can practically show how to get that way. I guess we shouldn't have been too surprised, since when the show started, we were told that we had to have twin beds for the Ricardos, even though the Arnazes were really married. Jess came up with the idea of having a priest, a rabbi, and a minister review the scripts. We wrote seven shows about Lucy having a baby, and nobody found anything objectionable.

The first show we did about the pregnancy was titled "Lucy is Enciente." We often borrowed words and situations from our families to use in the scripts. In this case, it was a word of Bob's mother, "dauncy," to describe when you aren't really sick but don't feel so hot. In the first scene of the show, Ethel comes into the kitchen to find Lucy dressed and on her way to the doctor.

ETHEL

What's the matter, honey? Are you sick?

LUCY

No, I just want to get a check-up. I've been feeling real dauncy.

ETHEL

Dauncy?

LUCY

That's a word my grandmother made up for when you're not really sick but you feel lousy.

ETHEL

Oh.

LUCY

I don't know what's the matter with me. I've been getting a lot of rest, but I don't have a lot of energy. I'm putting on a lot of weight. I just feel blaaah.

ETHEL

You probably need some vitamin pills or a liver shot or something.

LUCY

Yeah. Don't say anything to Ricky about my going to the doctor. No sense worrying him.

ETHEL

Okay.

LUCY

Gee whiz, I'm going to have to go on a diet. I could hardly get this dress on this morning.

ETHEL

(GETTING AN IDEA) Lucy, wait a minute. You don't suppose –

LUCY

I don't suppose what?

ETHEL

You don't suppose you're going to have a baby.

LUCY

Of course not. (DOES A TAKE) A baby?

Bob Carroll Jr. and Madelyn Pugh had a custom of giving a silver dollar for a job well done. Here they present a pregnant Lucy with hers for a great performance.

ETHEL

Yeah. That's a word my grandmother made up for little tiny people.

When I looked back in my old script to find the original dialogue for the scene, I was amazed to see it was written like this:

LUCY

I don't suppose what?

ETHEL

You don't suppose you're pregnant.

LUCY

Of course not. (TAKE) Pregnant?

ETHEL

Yeah. That's a word my grandmother made up when a woman is going to have a baby.

Apparently, we had written the script before the edict came down not to use the dreaded word, even though the original version was funnier. In those days without Xerox, we didn't have those different colored pages arriving every ten minutes, so we were supposed to write the changes in our scripts ourselves, which I guess I didn't bother to do.

Incidentally, Tom Watson, the president of Lucille Ball's fan club, tells me that he and his friends still use "dauncy" to describe their feelings when they have an off day.

Later in the show, Lucy is trying to find just the right tender moment to tell Ricky the great news. He is so busy she doesn't get a chance, so she goes to the Tropicana Nightclub, hoping somehow to tell him during rehearsal, but can't find a minute. So then she goes to the evening performance and has the maitre d' give him a note that says somebody in the audience is having a baby and would he please dedicate the next song to her. Ricky announces the news and starts walking around to the tables, singing "Rockabye Baby" so the lucky person will identify herself. When he gets to Lucy, she nods, and he does a big take and then sings to her. While he was singing, the Arnazes' own emotions came to the surface. They had waited so long to have children, and now they not only had one but were going to have a second one, and they both became tearful. Everyone in the control booth and the audience was crying, too. Billy Asher, the director, thought the scene had been ruined by all the tears, plus the fact that Desi was so excited he loused up the lyrics to "Rockabye Baby," so he shot the scene a second time. But when Billy saw the two versions in the editing room, he realized the first one was absolutely the one to air.

The show where the baby was actually born was called "Lucy Goes to the Hospital." It was planned for Lucille Ball to have her baby by Cesarean section. Lucy's physician, Dr. Joseph Harris, just happened to pick a Monday, so the real birth coincided with the birth of Lucy Ricardo's baby on the air. Earlier, Jess and Bob and I had to decide whether it was going to be a boy or a girl because this was before the days of amniocentesis, and you didn't know ahead of time. So we decided to make it a boy. We had a 50/50 chance of being right. The big event took place on January 19, 1953, and when Dr. Harris announced "it's a boy" and Desiderio Alberto Arnaz was born, a great shout went up in the delivery room. Meanwhile, Little Ricky was being born on TV. Newspapers carried banner headlines, and there were bulletins on news shows. The program received a Nielsen rating of 71.1, which represented about 44 million people.

Since there were only seven shows involving the pregnancy, we still had a lot more scripts to write for the second season, which aired thirty original programs. At the start of each season, Bob brought in a bunch of plastic numbers on a hook like the ones used in a deli and reversed them and hung them on the wall. So whenever we finished a script, we made a ceremony of taking off the number, which meant that we only had twenty-three or whatever to go. I'll admit it was something of a grind, but we were both young and single and worked all the time and, because of the hugely talented cast, it was mostly a lot of fun. The long hours cut down on our social life, but we sometimes dated each other so it worked out. Fortunately, we seldom had huge rewrites, and we didn't have much interference from the advertising agency or the network. Eddie Feldman of the Biow Agency came to rehearsals and hardly ever made suggestions. As he put it, "With ratings like yours, I'm going to tell *you guys* what to do?"

Lucy tells Ricky she is pregnant in "Lucy Is Enciente," and everyone is teary-eyed, including the studio audience.

Our routine would go like this: We would meet with the cast and the director on Monday morning and read the script around a table on the stage. They would begin rehearsing, and Bob and I would go to our office and start on the next script, which we had plotted with Jess the previous week. We attended a "run-through" late Tuesday afternoon and a dress rehearsal on Wednesday night, where we would all meet afterwards and discuss any problems. It was a group thing, and everybody was encouraged to give an opinion. Sometimes there were heated arguments, since everyone cared a lot about the show. Vivian was rather vocal, and Frawley would often doze off. We would make some changes, and on Thursday the cast would rehearse with the cameras and film the show in front of an audience that night.

On Friday, Jess, Bob, and I would get an idea for the story line for the week after next. Plotting day would begin with Bob and I having an early breakfast at the old Schwab's Drugstore on Sunset Boulevard because it was halfway between our homes. This is the famous Schwab's where supposedly somebody discovered Lana Turner while she was having a soda. (This site is now a mini-mall, as what isn't?) We kept a series of spiral notebooks in which we would write down one-line ideas of anything that would occur to us that we could use as a springboard for a script. We would go through these, pick out a couple, talk about how they might be developed, and then meet with Jess in his office or at his home. He would say, "What have you got?" and we would present him our choices, and then work with him to develop a story of five or six scenes. Jess, who had already taught us structure on *My Favorite Husband,* also taught us discipline. We had to get a story line completed by the end of the day or stay until midnight if it took that long. For some reason, when you know you have to get a story line by a certain time, you usually do.

I still have those tattered old spiral notebooks. We didn't use some of the ideas for various reasons. There was one notation, "Lucy's old boyfriend turns up, played by Frank Sinatra." This was highly optimistic since Mr. Sinatra didn't do roles on TV. Another idea was "Lucy raises chinchillas." This was during the time when it was still politically correct to wear a fur coat, and Lucy was always looking for ways to

Lucy and Bob Carroll Jr. compare beards during the shooting of "The Mustache" episode of I Love Lucy.

make extra money at home. Maybe we didn't do it because chinchillas are mean little critters or we couldn't find a chinchilla wrangler. Or maybe we didn't think it was very funny to discuss how you get their little skins off.

Another idea was to have Lucy visit her hometown of Jamestown, New York, and all her relatives look like her so she plays all the parts. Obviously, this was impossible to do in front of an audience because of all the hair and makeup changes, so it never happened. Another was for Lucy to make a roof garden on top of the apartment so Little Ricky will have a place to play. She goes through the roof into the ceiling of the Mertzes' apartment and Fred threatens to sue. Then there was one where the Ricardos and Mertzes decide to invest in property and buy a duplex together, and get into a big fight over how to redecorate. Well, not too many gems in there, but we were always thinking.

The third year of *Lucy* was filmed at Motion Picture Center Studios (later Desilu Cahuenga, then Renmar) and the offices were so small, Jess had a wall knocked down, combining two little rooms so his office was long and skinny. He liked to pace and jingle coins and keys in his pocket as he thought. While he walked the length of the office, Bob and I would sit on a couch at one end, and I would take rough notes. The schedule we were on didn't make us particularly bright-eyed, and Bob swears that he used to close his eyes and take a nap when Jess walked away from us, and open his eyes and look alert when Jess came back toward us.

So, now we had our story line and you know who (the girl writer) would type it up, and Bob and I would start on the script the next morning. We usually tried to have a small physical comedy routine for Lucy in the first act and a larger one for the ending of the show. Sometimes we got an idea for a big, broad routine for her and worked backwards, figuring how to get her in that predicament.

During the week, Jess would often call us and say, "How're you doing?" We would say, "Fine," and he would ask, "What page are you on?" We would pick a number, "17" or "28," when we were actually on page five because we didn't want to alarm him. Openings of scripts are hard. You have to plant the story line and come up with jokes and routines that have nothing to do with the plot. We usually spent all day on the first two or three pages. This, of course, is what gets cut when the show goes into syndication so they can put in more commercials. Recently, "Nick at Night" restored these scenes in *I Love Lucy*, for which we are eternally grateful. I was tickled to discover when I watched the PBS program *Caesar's Writers*, with the marvelous Sid Caesar and all his talented writers, they confessed how they did the same thing. Sid would come into the writers' room and look over the shoulder of whoever was typing the script to see what page they were on. They knew this, so they would write some big number like "33" when they were still on page seven.

Bob and I decided that we wasted a lot of time chatting about personal matters–what we called "going off on tangents"–which had nothing to do with the script. So we borrowed a jar from the prop department, one that said "Aunt Martha's Salad Dressing" from "The Million Dollar Idea" show, cut a hole in the lid, and made a pact that whoever started the tangent had to put in a quarter. But we argued so much over who really started the tangent that it took more time than before, so we had to abandon the plan.

Sometimes when we were working on a joke, we both talked at once, so we decided to try taping our writing sessions so as not to lose anything. We also thought we wasted a lot of time. What we found out was not only didn't we waste time, but we attacked a joke like a couple of pit bulls. So we also gave up the tape recorder.

We signed agreements with each other. Not your legal documents or anything, but apparently we were tired of hearing each other complain (did somebody say being a writing team is a lot like marriage?) and wanted to get things down on paper so we could hear the end of it.

Bob has saved some of these. There is one dated November 4, 1948. "I get sick from eating butter creams" with my signature. There is another, "Doughnuts give me indigestion," signed by me and dated October 6, 1950. I think this was after some midnight trips to the nearest all-night restaurant. And "I will not eat dinner before the show anymore because I get a stomach ache," signed January 19, 1983. I think I detect a trend here. Then there was this agreement: "Don't pat Madelyn on the rear in public," signed by Bob and dated October 14, 1949. There was also an agreement which went, "After five more shows, Bob Carroll Jr. may quit. During those five shows, Bob Carroll Jr. promises to never mention quitting again. He also promises to exhibit enthusiasm and, on occasion, to contribute material." This was signed by both of us, and dated April 17, 1957. I have no memory of what this was all about, but from the date, it must have been near the end of the season in the sixth year, and a certain ennui was setting in. I do remember one particular time when we were writing a scene, and Fred was supposed to come in the door with a funny line. Bob said, "Let Fred Mertz get his own joke."

Jess wanted each script finished to read over the weekend, so there was many a Saturday night at three in the morning when we drove to his house in Brentwood and left it in his mailbox. He would do a rewrite while we would start the process all over again.

I have to confess we never really liked Jess's rewrites. Most writers, of course, never like what other people do to their scripts. In my whole life, I have never heard a writer say, "Gee, thanks. Your rewrite sure improved my script a lot!" After a number of months, we felt we had to tell Jess. We were taking him to lunch at the Brown Derby for his birthday, and I am still embarrassed to confess that, with incredibly bad timing, we chose this occasion to tell him how we felt. At least we didn't sing, "Happy Birthday, dear Jess. Your rewrite's a mess." In his book, *Laughs, Luck and Lucy–How I Came to*

Create the Most Popular Sitcom of All Time, finished by his son Gregg Oppenheimer, he recalls our ill-timed complaints. He says he went through one of the scripts with us and carefully explained every single change he made and why. According to him, we still felt the same way. And I'm sure we did.

One of the shows we did during the third season was called "The Sentimental Anniversary" and came from the fact that the Arnazes were actually celebrating their 13th anniversary. They had a party on November 30, 1953, at a popular nightclub, The Mocambo on the Sunset Strip.

Bob and I were invited, and we wrote them a poem:

'Twas twenty-five days before Christmas
and all through The Mocambo
The creatures were stirring and doing the Mambo.
With Pa in his tux and Ma in her mink,
We'd just settled down for a long evening's drink,
When in the Champagne Room there arose such a clatter
We all ran in to see what was the matter.
And what to our wondering eyes did appear
A couple all full of anniversary cheer.
The man was so charming, so handsome and slick,
We knew from his accent he wasn't St. Nick.
And then in a twinkling, we saw by his side
A red-haired beauty who must be his bride.
Her eyes were so merry, so big and so blue,
It was really a shame she had only two.
The couple exhibited real wedded bliss,
Desi turned to Lucy and said with a kiss,
"These thirteen years, my love's grown stronger,"
"The way you say it," she said, "It sounds longer."
We're glad they're happy. We're glad they are one.
This poem took so long, this week's script isn't done.
But we'd like to exclaim as we slip out of sight,
Happy anniversary to you and to all a good night.

Tennessee Ernie Ford guest stars and Lucy tries to get rid of him by pretending to be a "Wicked City Woman."

Okay, it was corny, but it was hard to buy Lucy and Desi something they didn't already have, and anyway, we didn't have time to shop.

Also in the third season were a couple of shows called "Tennessee Ernie's Visit" and "Tennessee Ernie Hangs On" featuring Tennessee Ernie Ford. Ernie plays a distant rural cousin who drops in on the Ricardos unexpectedly and doesn't know when to leave. At the time, Ernie had a hilarious local radio show, but was just getting started in his career, so Lucy was not aware of him. When Bob and I walked on the set, even before he had read a line of dialogue, there was trouble brewing. Lucy took us aside. "This won't work," she announced. "He doesn't look like a hillbilly. With that little black mustache, he looks like a member of Desi's band." We were stricken. We had written the show especially for Ernie, even using some of his expressions like "pea-pickin'" and "for jumpin' up and down." I never knew if our guest star was aware of the turmoil behind the scenes. If he was, he just smiled and never let on. Jess decided since we were there and Ernie was there, we might as well have the reading of the script, so we did, and Tennessee Ernie had everybody screaming with laughter. Lucy told us, "I was wrong. He's wonderful!" He was so funny and the laughs made the show so long, we had to make it into a two-parter because she didn't want to cut anything. This was a classic example of how Lucy might flare up about something and make a snap judgment, but was never afraid to tell you later that she was wrong and apologize.

In coming up with ideas for the show, we always tried to start with a universal theme, something the audience could identify with and nod and say, "That same thing happened to me." Sometimes when we were looking for a new story line, Bob would say, "What'll we do this week? Jealousy? Greed? Envy? The men versus the women? Money?" We did a lot of shows where money was the theme–not having any, trying to get more, spending more than you should, and hiding it from your husband. Misunderstanding between friends is always good. One of the shows where we combined this with money was called "Never Do Business With Friends." The Ricardos had bought a new washing machine and sold their old one to the Mertzes. Of course, as soon as Ethel uses the machine, it breaks. Since Fred hasn't given Ricky his check for it yet, there is a big argument about who now owns the machine, with phrases like "unloading a lemon" and "welshing on a deal" being thrown about. Mrs. Trumbull, the Ricardos' babysitter (played by Elizabeth Patterson), hears about the problem and suggests that her nephew is a repairman and might be able to fix it. The repairman (Herb Vigran) arrives and offers to buy it for $50, which is $15 more than the original price. Now the couples argue over who owns the machine for a different reason, saying, "Friends are more important than a washing machine" and "A deal's a deal." They are dragging the machine back and forth toward their own doors on the back porch when they push it too close to the edge and it topples over the railing into the alley below. Now the argument starts all over again about exactly whose machine was just ruined.

This was the end of the original script that Bob and I wrote. Lucy didn't like the ending because she said each show should end happily. Bob and I liked the "here-we-go-again" kind of ending, but she was adamant. The ending was changed so that after the machine falls over the railing, and as they are all arguing, the repairman appears and says he's just talked to a friend who will now pay $75 for the machine. The group looks at each other, and all start to laugh at how ridiculous they have been. Ricky offers to split the cost of the broken railing with Fred, and everybody is satisfied. Now that I look back, I think Lucy was right about those happy endings. Bob always names this as his favorite show, I think maybe because selling something to a friend and having the situation get sticky is something that could happen to anybody.

SIX

California, Here We Come

TO GIVE THE SHOW A FRESH LOOK, WE DECIDED THE Ricardos and Mertzes would take a trip to Hollywood. We hoped this would be a universal theme that would appeal to viewers. Almost everyone has experienced the pitfalls of driving across the country, and almost everyone has been a tourist. And if they have been a tourist in Hollywood, they know that some of the highlights were (in those days) going to the Brown Derby, seeing the footprints in Grauman's Chinese Theater, visiting a movie set, trying to get autographs, and meeting stars. Wanting to meet stars still applies even today. There is hardly anyone so sophisticated that she wouldn't like to return from a visit to Hollywood and casually mention to her friends, "I was THIS close to Tom Hanks" or "I met Julia Roberts and she was just as nice as she could be."

The Ricardos and the Mertzes start out on their trip to California.

We did twenty-nine shows involving their trip to Hollywood. We aired twenty- three in the fourth season and saved six more to begin the fifth year. We hadn't planned to do so many, but the stories just seemed to keep on coming. We started out with Ricky getting an offer to be in a film, and he and Lucy plan to drive to California. At first, the Mertzes aren't going with them, and Ethel is bitterly disappointed. Lucy reassures her:

LUCY

Even after we win the Oscar, we'll still be the closest friends.

Ricky works it out so the Mertzes can go along, and the episodes include planning the trip; buying a car; driving across the country; visiting Tennessee Ernie Ford in Bent Fork, Tennessee; and stopping in Ethel's hometown, Albuquerque, New Mexico. And, of course, we had Lucy trying to get a part in a movie. Many of the episodes were about Lucy's and Ethel's efforts to meet movie stars. Every sitcom writer knows that having a guest star gives you new ideas for story lines, and we were lucky to get some great guests. The budget of the show didn't include the big salaries those actors usually received for their work, but we put in a plug for their current movie, and they had fun besides.

For the Hollywood shows, Pontiac supplied the car that the Ricardos and Mertzes drove across the country in exchange for the advertising. Bob and I had always heard about writers getting "freebies" because of what was written in the script, like mentioning Coca-Cola and then getting a free case of Coke every month or a free trip to Hawaii because the characters in the show were going to Honolulu on a vacation. But we never had seemed to get the hang of this. This time, though, we were going to get an honest-to-goodness freebie.

The plan was for the Mertzes and Ricardos to drive across country in Ricky's new Pontiac convertible. There were some exterior shots made of the car, with our editor Dann Cahn driving the car over the George Washington Bridge and going through Ohio, Tennessee, and on out west. The sponsor was generous enough to give Bob and me a new car to drive every three months, and we would trade in the old one. In the '50s, cars often had two-color paint jobs, so we'd check with each other. "What did you get this time?" "Mine's red and white. What did you get?" "Mine's white and black." At the end of the trip to Hollywood, Ricky sold the car and our group returned to Manhattan on the train, so Pontiac wasn't going to give us cars anymore. I got a call one morning from the local dealer. "We want the car," he said. I suspected this might be coming, so I told him, "Just let me buy a new car, and I'll turn this back to you." "Oh no," he said, "we want it now." And I had to get a ride home.

Fred eats while Lucy stares at Bill Holden through her makeup mirror in the Brown Derby Restaurant in "L.A. at Last!"

After an eventful trip across the country, the Ricardos and Mertzes arrived in California in an episode titled "L.A. at Last." They stayed at a fictional hotel called The Beverly Palm where you could see Vine Street and the Brown Derby sign out their window. They unpacked, Ricky went to have lunch at MGM, and Lucy and the Mertzes decided to hunt for movie stars.

LUCY

Tracking down movie stars one by one takes so much time. I wonder if there's any place where they get together in a big herd.

FRED

Well, maybe at sundown they all gather at the same watering hole.

LUCY

That's it! That's where we'll go!

ETHEL

Where?

LUCY

The watering hole. Fellow hunters, we're going to the Brown Derby!

So Lucy and the Mertzes go to the Brown Derby restaurant. The first celebrity they see is Eve Arden, who came over from the set next door where she was doing her series *Our Miss Brooks* to do the cameo. The maitre d' Gus (played by Harry Bartel) seats William Holden in the booth next to them. Lucy embarrasses herself, gawking at him and finally rushing out, bumping into a waiter, and causing him to dump a cream pie on Holden. Later, Holden meets Ricky at the studio and gives him a ride back to the hotel, and Ricky asks him to come up to the room to meet Lucy. Lucy doesn't want to ever see Holden again because of what happened at lunch, but Ricky insists. So Lucy covers her hair with a scarf, gets out Ricky's makeup case, and gives herself black eyebrows, glasses, and a putty nose as a disguise. Ricky is totally mystified and tries to carry it off. As Holden is lighting her cigarette, Lucy's nose, which she has pushed out of shape in her embarrassment, catches on fire. I wouldn't have blamed Lucy at all if she had refused to do the stunt, but as usual, she would do anything if it was funny.

When Lucy was interviewed on talk shows, and asked about that episode, she claimed it was a total accident and that when it happened, Bill Holden almost fainted. Well, not exactly. I can remember perfectly well when we first talked about doing the gag in Jess Oppenheimer's office and how he called Hal King, Lucy's makeup man, to see if he could construct a nose that could be set on fire without being dangerous to Lucy. I think Lucy told her version enough times that she believed it. It also made a better story. In

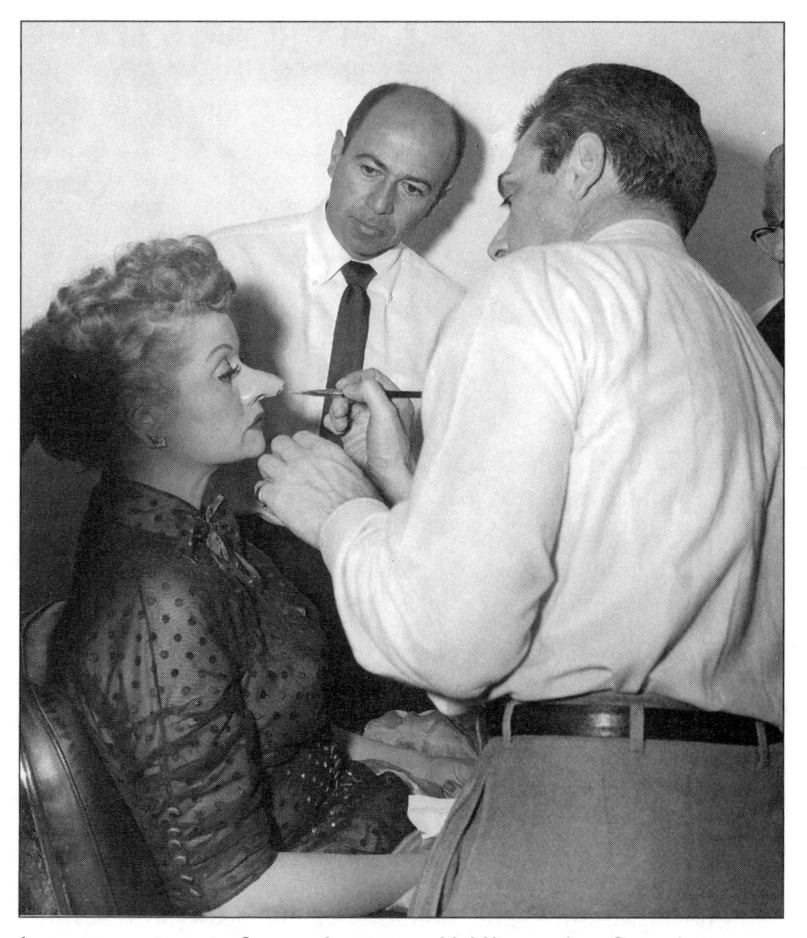

Lucy gets a new nose from make up man Hal King, as Jess Oppenheimer looks on.

reality, if Lucille Ball's nose accidentally caught on fire, Desi, Bill Holden, the director Bill Asher, and fifty other people would have rushed to her aid, and there would have been total pandemonium. As it was, everyone was collapsing with laughter. I checked the script, and this is how Lucy's "accident" was written:

LUCY TAKES BOTH HANDS AND TRIES TO STRAIGHTEN HER NOSE OUT, AND MAKES IT

COME TO MORE OF A POINT THAN EVER. RICKY AND HOLDEN LOOK AT HER, VERY PUZZLED, AND SHE TRIES TO COVER HER EMBARRASSMENT BY PICKING UP A CIGARETTE BOX.

LUCY

Cigarette, anybody?

THEY ALL TAKE ONE, INCLUDING LUCY. HOLDEN PICKS UP A TABLE LIGHTER, GETS UP TO LIGHT LUCY'S CIGARETTE, AND HER NOSE CATCHES ON FIRE. THE END OF THE NOSE STARTS TO FLAME AND SMOKE, AND SHE QUICKLY GRABS IT OFF AND DROPS THE NOSE IN HER COFFEE CUP.

This is exactly the way it was performed, with one exception. Instead of taking off the nose and dropping it in the coffee cup, Lucy lifted the cup and put out the fire by dipping her nose in it like a bird, making it much funnier.

Bill Holden and Lucy had worked together in movies, and they were great together. We plugged his movie *The Country Girl* in which he starred with Grace Kelly, who won the Academy Award for her role. Milt Josefsberg, who wrote for Lucy years later and was then working for Jack Benny's TV show, said that Jack borrowed a print of this show and ran it for his writers.

Before "L.A. at Last!" was shown on the air, a party was held in a private room of the Brown Derby in Hollywood for the big columnists and show biz writers so they could preview the show. After cocktails and hors d'oeuvres were served, the lights dimmed and then there was a long, awkward pause. The projector wouldn't work. Every man in the room must have taken a try at fixing it, but it still wouldn't work. Incidentally, women who want to meet men are missing a good bet. Just stand by some mechanical object—a car, a

Lucy accidentally sets fire to her own nose while Bill Holden and Ricky react.

computer, whatever—and say "This doesn't work," and men will leap out of the bushes to fix it. I once picked up the phone and, hearing no dial tone, said "This doesn't work." My husband and two of my sons each went over and jiggled the receiver to be sure I hadn't made a mistake. The projector never did work that night, and Desi was so angry I thought he might implode.

Desi's temper was legendary, but Bob and I were lucky. In all those years, he never yelled at us. We weren't very confrontational, and if yelling started anywhere, we both reacted by seeming to disappear—sometimes to another country. One day at a meeting, some poor soul incurred Desi's wrath by doing something wrong or forgetting to do something right. The meeting was almost over, and Bob and I didn't see any reason why we had to stay for this unpleasant scene, so we started tiptoeing toward the door. Desi looked up, stopped yelling and said in a perfectly normal voice, "See you later, kits," and went back to hollering. When he became angry, his eyes did bug out, and you could see the veins in his forehead, like we used to make jokes about in the scripts.

We used our recurring theme of Lucy trying to get into show business in a script called "Lucy Gets in Pictures." Ricky is working in his movie, the Mertzes get a two-week job in a movie directed by an old pal of theirs, and even the bellboy (played by Bobby Jellison) has one line in a picture. Lucy feels so left out that Ricky, against his better judgment, asks a director to give her a tiny role that turns out to be one where she has no lines and is killed in the very first scene.

Lucy is to play a chorus girl in one of those old musicals where beautiful girls walked around in skimpy costumes and huge, towering headdresses. Someone shoots her as she parades down a flight of stairs. Well, you only have to think of Lucy in an enormous, heavy headdress that keeps throwing her off balance, trying to walk down a long flight of stairs, to imagine what she would do with it, and she was great. After ruining three takes, the director (played by Lou Krugman, a fine character actor who appeared on the show a lot) loses patience and gives her heavy headdress to another bigger girl. Lucy and Lou had a little gem of a scene because of the way they played it, where they are sitting on the steps and he is trying to explain that he is on a budget and has to get this scene shot. Lucy explains that she can't go home and face her friends without having been in the movies and to please give her another chance.

LUCY

But wouldn't you like to see me die?

DIRECTOR

Don't tempt me.

The director has the other girl play the murder victim, and

Lucy is just a member of the chorus. When the shot rings out and the other girl gets hit, Lucy reacts anyway and staggers to her death down the long flight of stairs. The director, near the end of his rope, asks Lucy why she did this.

DIRECTOR

Mrs. Ricardo, what do you think you're doing? That shot was supposed to be for the other girl!

LUCY

Well, he missed!

In one of the other episodes, Lucy, star-struck as usual, finds out that Cornel Wilde is staying in the hotel suite right above them. She finds a way to sneak into his room just to get a glimpse of him and gets trapped and has to hide on the balcony. She then (what else?) gets locked out and has to make a rope ladder to try to swing down into her own room below. Ricky comes home while this is going on, and Ethel tries to stall about where Lucy is. Vivian's reaction when she sees Lucy plummet past the balcony is classic comedy. Throughout all the shows, Ethel's reaction of what Lucy is doing, or about to do, made it that much funnier. Someone once asked Lucy if she ever watched any of her old shows, and she said, "Sometimes. And when I do, I watch Viv."

At this point, the Ricardos and Mertzes have been together an awful lot—riding in the car across country and having hotel rooms right down the hall from each other, so they were starting to get on each other's nerves a little. We did a show called "In Palm Springs" that started with the foursome complaining about various little habits they each had. Just between us, we based these habits on some that were very close to home. Ricky's annoying habit was to nervously tap his fingers, which was a thing Bob did that sometimes drove me crazy. Fred jingled his keys and coins in his pocket, something Jess did when we were working on a story. Lucy stirred her coffee endlessly, which Jess and Bob claimed (without foundation) that I did. Ethel's bad habit was eating noisily and smacking her lips over food, and I have mercifully forgotten who we based that on. The foursome become quite miffed with each other for pointing out these social lapses, and they decide they need some time away from each other. Lucy and Ethel go to Palm Springs for the weekend, and Ricky and Fred stay at the hotel. Naturally, the women missed their husbands, even with their annoying habits, and the men start getting on each other's nerves and miss their wives, or as Ricky put it:

RICKY

Well, it may sound crazy, but think it over. We miss our wives.

FRED

Oh, come now.

RICKY

Sure we do. I really miss Lucy.

FRED

You don't suppose I miss Ethel?

RICKY

Why else would you be so cranky and irritable?

FRED

My liver could be out of whack.

(Your liver being out of whack was one of Bob's mother's expressions.)

The men decide to go to Palm Springs and surprise their wives. When they get there, they run into Rock Hudson and put him up to telling Lucy and Ethel a sad story about a couple named Adell and Sam who split up because of the husband's bad habit of whistling through his teeth absent-mindedly.

ROCK

Sam would (WHISTLES) all day and (WHISTLES) all night and finally Adell couldn't stand it anymore. She said, 'Sam, just one more (WHISTLES), and I'll leave you.'

LUCY

And?

ROCK

And he (WHISTLES), and she did.

LUCY

She did? She left him?

ROCK

She left him.

LUCY

Just because of one (WHISTLES)?

ETHEL

They'll probably get together again.

LUCY

Yes, if you love a person, you shouldn't let a little (WHISTLES) come between you.

Rock explains that Sam was in an accident, and Adell rushed to the hospital and hoped to hear Sam speak to her one last time, but by the time she got there it was too late.

LUCY

No more (WHISTLES)?

ROCK

No more (WHISTLES). Sam will never (WHISTLES) again.

By now, Lucy and Ethel are in tears at this sad story.

Ricky and Fred appear, admit they put Rock up to it, and the couples make up.

In another of our Hollywood shows, Harpo Marx was the guest. The story line was that Lucy has written to her friend Carolyn Appleby (played by Doris Singleton) and bragged about how many big stars she has met in Hollywood. Unexpectedly, Carolyn arrives on a visit and wants to meet some of Lucy's new celebrity pals. Lucy is in a jam, so she hides Carolyn's glasses so she can't see clearly and dresses like Harpo in his traditional baggy jacket, blond wig, and battered hat.

Meanwhile, the real Harpo drops by, prompted by Ricky, and when he sees Lucy, he thinks he must be looking in a mirror. He keeps doing physical things to prove he isn't seeing double, and Lucy pops out from behind the door and mimics his every move. When we wrote the script, we had put in the directions that when Lucy sees the real Harpo enter, she hides out on the balcony of the hotel room, upstage, and they do a routine there. Bill Asher, the director, changed the staging, having Lucy hide behind a folding door to the kitchenette, downstage. Billy was absolutely right as this worked much better for both the cameras and the studio audience.

At the end of the routine, Harpo drops his hat and so does Lucy, only Harpo has his hat on a rubber band, and it pops up again, and Lucy's hat doesn't, and that's how he catches her. Lucy and Harpo worked on the pantomime routine tirelessly in rehearsal so it would be perfect, and it was. And of course, this wasn't done with any trick photography or computer graphics, but filmed in front of an audience in one take. It was a rare privilege to see these two comedy legends work together.

In their pursuit of seeing stars, Lucy and Ethel took a bus tour of the movie stars' homes. Bob and I took one of those tours to see what ideas we could get. One of the things of interest we saw was the mailbox in front of Shirley Temple's old house, shaped like her doll house, which we mentioned in the script. The tour went to Richard Widmark's home, and Lucy sees a grapefruit on a tree in the yard, which would make the perfect souvenir. She talks the bus driver into stopping, and in reaching for the grapefruit, falls over the wall into Widmark's yard and can't get out. Lucy needed the grapefruit to go along with the orange she has that was signed by Robert Taylor when she saw him in the Farmer's Market. She talked him into autographing the orange since she forgot to bring along a paper and pen. In our original script, the orange was signed by Cary Grant. Later in the same script, it was changed to Jimmy Stewart. When we did the show on the air, it turned out it was Robert Taylor. I have no idea why the names were changed, but that orange sure got around.

Lucy's determination to get the souvenir to end all souvenirs was the episode that opened the fifth season as she and Ethel stole the block of cement that contained John Wayne's footprints from the forecourt of Grauman's Chinese Theater. James Kern was our director for that year, and two new writers were added—a team of nice, talented guys, Bob Schiller and Bob Weiskopf. When Jess told us that they were to join us, we were thrilled. More writers, hooray! There was talk of calling us "Three Bobs and a Babe," but fortunately that never caught on.

Bob Carroll and I went to Grauman's Chinese Theater (now Mann's) and gawked at all the celebrity footprints, and the four of us wrote the script together with Jess. The story was that Lucy and Ethel notice John Wayne's slab is loose on one side, and they plan to come back late at night, steal the slab, and fill in the empty space with a bucket of wet cement they bring with them. The plans go awry, and Lucy ends up with her foot firmly encased in a bucket of hard cement. They are working on getting the bucket off her foot in the Mertzes' hotel room when Ricky arrives home and they jump into bed and cover everybody with blankets. Ricky tries to talk Lucy into coming back to their hotel room, then finally picks her up, cement and all, and the blankets fall off.

RICKY

Okay, let's have the story.

LUCY

Story? What makes you think there's a story?

RICKY

Well, the Mertzes are in bed with their clothes on and you have your foot stuck in what seems to be a block of cement...I just thought there might be some explanation.

LUCY

You'd think so, wouldn't you?

John Wayne appeared in the second show of this two-part episode. The comedy scene he and Lucy have together includes Lucy sneaking into his dressing room at the studio to borrow a pair of his boots. She ends up having to pretend to be a masseur and gives Wayne a rubdown. Wayne made a joke during rehearsal when he took off his bathrobe, saying he hoped the camera wouldn't take a close-up of any flab he might have. He didn't really have any. Even though he played mostly dramatic parts in the movies, he turned out to have a flair for comedy. To get him to do the show, we plugged *Blood Alley,* his current picture, not exactly his best effort, but who cared, we got Duke as a guest star.

Ricky decides they should sell the car and go back to New York on the train. We called this show "The Great Train Robbery." Lou Krugman played a jewel thief, and Frank Nelson was the long-suffering conductor. The show was technically difficult to produce because Lucy pulls the emergency brake, and the entire train shudders to a stop—

three times. The train was mounted on springs, so when Lucy pulled the brake, the entire set pitched forward. Our special effects men were fabulous. When Jess or Desi asked them if they could do the wild things we dreamed up, in front of an audience, they always figured it out and did it beautifully. They never once said, "You've got to be kidding!"

SEVEN

You Wouldn't Fit In, You're a Girl

When I was starting out and there weren't very many women comedy writers around, I don't remember concentrating on being a pioneer, like "I think I'll break some ground here." That's just the way it was. I was determined to be some kind of writer and have a career back in the days when that was considered sort of weird. Was there discrimination against women? Well, yeah. I think I didn't exactly fight it, I just acted like I didn't know it was there. As soon as I teamed up with a male partner, I seemed to become more acceptable. Also, since Lucille Ball was a woman, it didn't make much sense to say they didn't want a female writer on the show.

I guess people didn't know what to make of me. One interviewer described me as being "ladylike," and another said I didn't look like a comedy writer, I looked like a PTA president. I must have left my fake black mustache and big floppy shoes at home that day.

Before I started writing with Bob, there was one infamous moment when I was struggling to get on a network radio show. I applied to a young male comedy team who were planning a pilot. They were very polite but explained that they weren't going to hire me because "you wouldn't fit in, you're a girl." I proved that I was just as good as the next guy by going to the ladies' room and bursting into tears.

At the time I was trying to get started, for some reason females were asked to sit in the back of the comedy bus. In the early days of movies, women writers like Frances Marion, Adela Rogers St. Johns, and Anita Loos churned out innumerable comedies. Frances Marion wrote more than one hundred scripts and also produced some of them, winning two Academy Awards. Somewhere along the line, we seem to have dropped the ball. In the early 1950s, there were only a handful of "girl writers" doing comedy. I was in Hollywood, along with Peggy Chantler and Irma Kalish. Irma was writing with her husband Austin, often called Rocky, for the *Colgate Comedy Hour* starring Dean Martin and Jerry Lewis. Lucille Kallen and Selma Diamond were writing in New York.

On *Lucy*, there was some talk of my being an asset because I had "the woman's point of view," whatever that was. The comedy writer Laura Levine told me she had a similar thing happen. She was hired to write four scripts for *The Bob Newhart Show* because they wanted the feminine viewpoint on some episodes featuring "Emily," Bob's wife, played by Suzanne Pleshette. One of my unspoken functions on the Lucy shows was to keep an eye on Lucy's wardrobe. Not the costumes like the gypsy queen or the grape-stomper or the candy maker, but the ordinary day-to-day outfits. I was the one who had to sidle over to her and say, "Uh—when you do that stunt,

Producer Jess Oppenheimer, Madelyn, and Bob confer with the new writers, Bob Weiskopf and Bob Schiller.

you'd better wear pants because the camera can see up your skirt" and that sort of valuable information. Lucy had an excellent, long-legged figure and had once modeled for the designer Hattie Carnegie in New York, but to be perfectly frank, she didn't seem to have a great clothes sense. Elois Jenssen and Eddie Stevenson, costume designers for the show, and Della Fox, wardrobe person, did their best, but she often brought some little number that she was fond of from home, much to their despair. We all worked with her for years, but we never quite got the hang of discussing her wardrobe. If one of us didn't care for a particular outfit, Lucy would say, "It's the only one I have," like a battalion of wardrobe people and seamstresses weren't standing by to go shopping or whip something together. It wasn't that we were critical. Well, we *were* critical, but we wanted her to look just right.

Early, I thought perhaps Desi could be my ally in monitoring her wardrobe, and it might be more tactful coming from him. During dress rehearsal on one show, Lucy appeared in a navy jacket, white pleated skirt, and flats, which I think was her idea of what to wear in a scene on shipboard. Now any woman knows that a white skirt with box pleats is a no-no unless you're 5'10" and model thin. I murmured to Desi that I thought the outfit made Lucy look fat. He spoke up loudly in front of the whole cast and crew, saying, "Honey, Madelyn thinks that skirt makes you look fat." So much for that idea.

Another time, I was designated to tell her that some creation of hers wasn't quite making it. I don't recall the outfit, but I remember rehearsing my approach. I planned to say something like, "The only thing worse than telling a woman her dog has been run over is telling her you don't like her dress." Okay, so it was a dumb idea, but it seemed diplomatic at the time. I went to her dressing room, and I got as far as "The only thing worse than telling a woman her dog has been run over…" and Lucy, the animal lover, leaped up, "What woman? What dog? What happened??" Somehow, the critique of the dress never got back on track.

But before women writers became wardrobe consultants and necessary evils because we knew what women characters were thinking, the comedy writing business was really a men's club. Maybe it was because in radio and early TV, so many of the stars were former nightclub comics and vaudevillians and were used to the days when they would walk out the stage door where guys were hanging around trying to sell them a joke for ten bucks. When I went on staff at CBS, I shared an office with Kathleen Hite, the first woman writer ever hired there, and we became best friends. She was very witty and said funny things all the time, but she wrote drama. My credits were all comedy, but as someone once remarked

Madelyn and Bob lean out their window at Desilu-Gower Studios looking for women writers.

to me, "I can't believe you're a comedy writer. You haven't said anything funny all evening."

Kathleen eventually wrote a lot of action dramas (more than sixty *Gunsmoke* episodes), *Laramie, Wagon Train,* and created *Empire.* One of her favorite reactions to her being a woman writer was when she entered a producer's office with the script she had just finished for a private-eye TV series starring Dick Powell. The producer remarked jocularly, "What's a nice girl like you doing in a place like this?" This is not to be confused with the line Kathleen and I heard many times as we toiled in radio and TV, "How come a nice girl like you isn't married?" Neither one of us ever found a witty put-down for that one.

Actually, Kathleen started at CBS as a secretary, which was odd because she didn't learn shorthand on purpose since she really didn't want to become a secretary, and knowing how to take dictation was one of those skills you needed in those days. I, on the other hand, learned to take shorthand because I figured I could always start as a secretary and go on to better things.

Kathleen had an interview with Frances Wilder, head of personnel, CBS West Coast. She announced she wanted to be a writer, and Frances told her CBS didn't hire women writers. She said she didn't agree with the policy, but that's the way it was. But she must have sensed Kathleen's ability somehow because she offered her a job as her secretary. Kathleen explained she didn't want to be a secretary, and Frances told her the only way she could make it was to start from within. "But I don't know shorthand," Kathleen said, and Frances said, "I'll talk slow."

Kathleen was a non-shorthand-taking secretary for about six months, leaving samples of her writing on the desks of John Dunkel and Tommy Tomlinson, the heads of the writing staff, and was hired as a junior writer at $37.50 a week. When you became a senior writer, you made $57.50 a week, plus small fees if you wrote a show that had a sponsor. And when you stop shaking your head in amazement, I should add that writers were paid those high prices because the Writers Guild had struck a hard bargain. Kathleen was pleased because her first job was at a small radio station in

Wichita, Kansas, and she swore her starting salary was $3.50 a week to cover her lunch money.

Irma Kalish meanwhile was doing the same thing, hoping to be a writer, but taking shorthand in college just in case. She worked as a secretary on a magazine in New York, slipping her short stories to various editors and eventually selling them and being paid two cents a word. Irma later wrote more than 300 TV scripts for comedy shows like *All in the Family, The Bob Newhart Show, Maude,* and *The Brian Keith Show.* Her producing credits include *Good Times, Too Close for Comfort,* and *The Facts of Life.* She says she once went to a script meeting, and as she was leaving with her co-writer husband, Rocky, she heard someone say, "She must do the typing."

Peggy Chantler came to Hollywood in the late '40s as a Bergen scholar. Young writers were hired as apprentices on the *Edgar Bergen and Charlie McCarthy* radio show and paid $75 a week for six weeks. (Remember Edgar Bergen, Candice's father?) If at that time the young writers decided to go back home, the show paid their train fares. Peggy opted to stay, and one of her first jobs was as an "idea" person on the West Coast audience participation show named *Meet the Missus.* Peggy told me she thought up the "fun" spot on the show. For instance, two people would be brought up from the audience where an important question would be settled like, "Can you eat a plate of spaghetti faster with your fork or your fingers?" The winner got a prize. Peggy often teamed with William Cowley and her credits included the sitcoms *Hazel, The Donna Reed Show, The Courtship of Eddie's Father,* and *Dennis the Menace.* Peggy said she was never aware of much prejudice because she was a woman, but on one show when she was the script editor, the executive producer held a meeting to discuss where the show was headed and not only didn't invite her, but barred her from the all-male room. She said she quietly cleaned out her desk and went home.

Meanwhile, women were starting to politely claw their way to the top of the executive ladder. Ethel Winant became vice president of casting for CBS and was later named "Producer of the Year" by the Producers Guild of America. In an interview she gave to the Television Academy's Foundation Archives, she told the story about how, in the early days, just off the executive dining room, there was a bathroom, and it didn't have a lock (they were all men, so who needed a lock?). She got tired of going down two floors to the ladies' room, so whenever she used the executive one, she would leave her shoes outside the door to signal that a woman was inside.

After she was made vice president, she attended her first annual board meeting, and William Paley, president of CBS, had flown out from New York for the occasion. He was opening his mail and handed it to her, saying, "Here, would you make sure my secretary gets this?" She said there was a split second when she wondered what to do, and then she said, "Mr. Paley, the butler is right behind you, why don't you give your mail to him?" He handed the mail to the butler and gave her a look that said, "You give them a title and look what happens!"

Kathleen Hite and I broke the gender barrier at CBS, and shortly after that they hired a third woman, dramatic writer Beth Barnes. The three of us would come to work dressed in suits and high heels, perfect examples of what were known then as "career women." I mentioned this to Dana Reston, a writer on *Home Improvement,* telling her that I had seen *Laughter on the 23rd Floor,* a Broadway comedy by Neil Simon, based on the talented group of writers who wrote for Sid Caesar on TV. "I loved it," I told her, "and I laughed so hard because the sole woman writer on the staff came to work in a little suit and pumps just like I used to." She looked at me in amazement and asked, "Did they *make* you dress like that?"

Lucille Kallen, who was the only woman on the staff of *Your Show of Shows* starring Caesar and Imogene Coco, has told me that the character in the Simon play was based loosely on a combination of her and Selma Diamond. Selma was a very funny person and later became a comedy actor. Probably her best-known role was as a court officer, Selma Hacker, in the TV series *Night Court.* I always liked her line, "I want to live to the age of 90 and be shot by a jealous lover." Leonard Stern, producer-writer, remembers working with Selma on *The Honeymooners* with Jackie Gleason. He said she had the flu, but lay down on the office floor and pitched jokes because she was afraid if she didn't show up for work, she would get fired. She also worked on *Caesar's Hour, The Edie Adams Show,* and wrote for Milton Berle.

Lucille Kallen began in television in 1949 when she and her partner, Mel Tolkin, wrote all thirty-nine of the scripts for a season of *The Admiral Broadway Revue.* She and Mel then did material for *Your Show of Shows.* She told me they would write the sketches, and then the show was put together with all the pantomime bits and other business by the whole writing staff. She says the "Writers' Room" was actually the office of the producer, Max Liebman. It was 14' x 20' with one window that was always shut, and she was working with six men who smoked cigars. She not only developed headaches, but had trouble getting heard, since all the men were rather loud. At one point, she brought in a red scarf and when she had an idea, she would stand up on the couch and wave her scarf to get their attention.

Lucille also told me that in one job interview, a producer asked her, "Do you put out?" She said she burst out laughing and didn't get the job. I was so naïve back in those days, if someone had asked me if I put out, I would have said yes, thinking they were talking about the trash.

The gang is all prepared for Lucy to go to the hospital to have her baby, until Lucy actually says "It's time."

Bob Carroll and I never worked in a room with a large group that way. Today, the "Writers' Room" has come back in vogue, and the show runner is in charge, with all the staff sitting around pitching ideas and gags. Liz Sage, a comedy writer who has written on various sitcoms, told me that if you work in the "Writers' Room" and you're a woman, there is often an atmosphere of being in a men's locker room. When it gets too gross, you have to speak up and say, "Hey, guys, come on!"

Linda Morris, who writes with her husband, Vic Rauseo, told me that at one time she was working with a male producer-writer, and when she offered an idea, he would answer by speaking to Vic, as if she were invisible. Irma Kalish also had the problem of being The Invisible Woman. She said she and her husband Rocky were writing on a sitcom, and the star always talked right through her to

Rocky, never addressing her directly. One time Rocky was off somewhere and wasn't on the set. She said the star came toward her and she thought, "Ah ha! He's finally going to speak right to me." And he did. He came up to her and said, "Where's Rocky?"

Everybody has their stories. I'm not sure if this one should be filed under "discrimination" or "huh?" Bob and I wrote a script for a movie (which was never made) for an independent producer. We were having a conference about rewrites with the producer and some of his staff (all men). He taped our comments and later had the tape transcribed. The men, including Bob, were identified on tape. I was called "Woman Whoever She Is."

I thought perhaps this ignoring of women was some sort of aberration because comedy writing has always been looked on as a guy thing. But then I read *Personal History*, the autobiography of Katharine Graham, the celebrated publisher of *The Washington Post*. In her book, she described how she was quite often the only woman at a meeting, and she wrote, "I often discovered that at times women were invisible to men, who looked through you as though you weren't there."

With all the advances made by women in TV and film through the years, I assumed that the invisibility factor was a thing of the past. But recently, in *Written By*, the magazine of The Writers Guild of America, West, Susan Bullington Katz interviewed Marta Kauffman, the creator, with her partners David Crane and Kevin Bright, of the TV show *Friends* and other hit series. When she was asked if it was a big deal being a female writer, Marta replied, "It's a huge deal. I am treated differently. I mean, there are people who, in a conversation with Kevin and David and me, won't look at me. They will look at them and literally don't see me."

In my many years of writing, when I felt discriminated against because I was a woman, it was so dumb, it was kind of funny. I mean, a writer is a writer, isn't she/he? I never got to the point that Selma Diamond claimed she did when late one night she and a group of male writers finished a script. One of the men suggested, "Why don't we celebrate and go out on the town?" Selma said she heard herself saying, "Good idea. Where can we find some girls?"

EIGHT

Bon Voyage

In the fifth season of *I Love Lucy,* the Ricardos came home from Hollywood, and we did several domestic episodes and then, to keep things interesting, we had them take another trip, this time to Europe for a tour of Ricky's band. I remember sitting in a room with Jess and the three Bobs and discussing what we would do for the coming year and somebody said, "Hey, why don't we take them to Europe?" It was probably Bob Carroll, who went to Europe every chance he got. So Lucy and Ricky planned another trip with the usual skirmishes over who is going on the trip and who isn't. Ricky solves the problem by hiring Fred as the band manager so the Mertzes can afford to go along. There are some tense moments when Lucy can't find her birth certificate and so can't get a passport. She plans to stow away in an old steamer trunk, and when she tries the stunt out, she gets locked in the trunk with the key in her pocket (doesn't everybody?).

Ricky has planned to travel by ship with his band playing en route, and naturally Lucy misses the boat, having gotten off to give one more kiss to Little Ricky, who is on the dock with Lucy's mother (played by Kathryn Card). Lucy also misses the tugboat and has to arrive on the ship by helicopter. Again, the special effects department outdid themselves, and a brave Lucille Ball was lowered in a harness from the top of the stage. Believe me, that's a loooong way down to the floor when you're the one who has to do it.

When the Ricardos and Mertzes arrive in Paris, Lucy wants to act like a real native and not an American tourist, so she goes out to see the city on her own. She buys a painting from a sidewalk artist (played by Shep Menken) and decides to have lunch at a little sidewalk café. She orders escargot by mistake, and when she discovers they are snails, she addresses them:

LUCY

I think an American cousin of yours ate my geraniums.

She then tries to eat one by putting snail tongs on her nose so she won't have to taste anything. Earlier in the episode, she has unwittingly exchanged her American dollars for counterfeit francs. Now, as she is trying to leave the café, the counterfeit money is discovered, and Lucy ends up in jail. Ricky arrives to straighten things out, but it is very complicated because he and Lucy don't speak French. Finally, there is a "translation" routine where the gendarme who arrested her and speaks only French asks questions of another gendarme, who speaks French and German, who translates by talking to a prisoner who speaks German and Spanish, who translates to Ricky who speaks Spanish and English, who translates to Lucy. Then the answer goes back

Lucy visits her first Paris café, orders escargot, and is surprised when they turn out to be snails.

through the chain of translation again and another question is asked, and so on back and forth. Bud Molin, who was our film editor for the third season through the sixth, came to us with this idea. He recently reminded me that the routine was such a hit, we rewarded him with a silver dollar, which he still has. Bob and I had developed a tradition of awarding silver dollars when someone had contributed a particularly

Lucy ends up in a French jail and tries to explain how she wound up with counterfeit money.

fine job of acting or makeup or props. Lucy, of course, had a big collection of silver dollars, and the only trouble was one night when we didn't give her a dollar, she thought we didn't like her performance.

Another show we did while the Ricardos and Mertzes were in Europe starred the French-born movie idol Charles Boyer, who was just as charming and sexy as he seemed on the screen, and was a good sport, too. At one point, Lucy (thinking he is a Charles Boyer look-alike) makes fun of his accent, inadvertently squirts ink on his shirt, rips his coat up the back, and sits on his hat. We also did an episode based in London about Lucy's efforts to meet the Queen, another where she is in a fox hunt, and a dream sequence while they were in Scotland, with music by Eliot Daniel and lyrics by Larry Orenstein.

While they were in Lucerne, the foursome took a hike

in the Swiss Alps. As comedy writers know, confinement is a good device. Put people in a spot where they're trapped and don't know if they're ever going to get out alive, and inevitably they will start confessing secrets to each other, secrets that when they do get out, they're really sorry they brought up. In "Lucy in the Swiss Alps," written by the three Bobs, Jess, and me, the Ricardos and Mertzes are caught in a snow storm and take refuge in a small ski hut. Lucy accidentally slams the door and the snow cascades off the roof, blocking the door, and they can't get out.

FADE IN ON THE INTERIOR OF A SMALL SHACK WITH A SLANTED CEILING. THERE IS NO FURNITURE. OUR FOURSOME HAS BEEN HERE FOR SOME TIME. THEY ARE PACING NERVOUSLY IN DIFFERENT DIRECTIONS, JUST MISSING EACH OTHER AS THEY PASS. THERE IS A LOOK OF UTTER DESPERATION ABOUT OUR LITTLE GROUP.

LUCY

Oh dear, we're never going to get out of here.

RICKY

Now, now, honey.

ETHEL

She's right. I think we're doomed.

RICKY

Don't talk like that.

LUCY

I wouldn't believe it would end like this. (SOBS) I'm too young to go.

ETHEL

So am I.

FRED

Oh, come now, Ethel.

RICKY

Now, get hold of yourselves.

LUCY THROWS HER ARMS AROUND RICKY AND SOBS. ETHEL DOES THE SAME THING WITH FRED. FRED AND RICKY CONSOLE THE GIRLS BY PATTING THEM GENTLY ON THEIR BACKS.

ETHEL

Well, if this is really it and I've got to go, I want to go with a clear conscience, Fred. I have a confession to make to you.

FRED

What is it, honeybunch?

ETHEL

Well, (SOB) remember when we got married... I said I was eighteen?

FRED

Yeah?

ETHEL

I was nineteen.

FRED

I've got something to tell you, too.

ETHEL

What?

FRED

You were twenty-four.

LUCY AND RICKY LAUGH.

FRED (CONT'D)

Well, while we're on the subject, I might as well confess to you and Lucy.

RICKY

Confess what?

FRED

For the last three years, I've been charging you ten dollars a month more rent than anyone else in the building.

ETHEL

I've got another confession to make, Fred. Every month I gave them back the ten dollars.

FRED

What? Oh, if I knew I was going to get out of here, would I let you have it!

LUCY

Ricky, have you got anything to confess?

RICKY

Nope. I'm no fool. We might get saved.

LUCY

Well, I have a confession. I have another whole sandwich left in my knapsack.

RICKY

Now that I think of it, I have a confession to make. While you were napping, we ate it!

When the group traveled to Rome, we did an episode "Lucy's Italian Movie" that seems to be one of the public's favorites. Jess had a theory that he called "the suspension of disbelief," that is, the viewer would go along with any of Lucy's wild schemes if you started with an ordinary problem and then led them step by step, and make it clear that when she got in a jam, she didn't have any other choice. We would often have Ricky ask her, "Are you crazy or somethin'?" Or we would have Ethel say about one of Lucy's schemes, "That's the dumbest thing I ever heard of" and Lucy would answer, "You got a better idea?" We hoped in this way to tell the viewer that we knew it was crazy, too, but Lucy was

Bob Carroll Jr. in fez is an extra at the roulette wheel in Monte Carlo.

desperate and it *might* work. Lucy would then talk Ethel into helping her, often using a little blackmail. We tried to cover holes in the story by having our characters question things before the viewer did. The Italian movie story (directed by James Kern) was one where Lucy is going to have a bit part in a movie entitled *Bitter Grapes* because at the time there was a popular Italian movie called *Bitter Rice.* Lucy wants to soak up local color for the role, or as Desi referred to it, "Suck up luckal color." We knew by that time they had more modern methods of making wine than by stamping grapes with their bare feet (but they're not as funny), so we checked into it and found that they still stamped grapes in some small Italian villages. We covered it by Lucy getting information from the bellboy at the hotel in Rome:

LUCY

I'd like to know a bit about the wine industry.

How they make the wine, how they pick the grapes, how they press the juice out with their feet. Are there any grape vineyards around here?

BELLBOY

There is only one little town where they do that anymore. All the other wineries are modern and use machinery.

LUCY

Is this town very far away?

BELLBOY

No. It's called Turo—it's right outside of town.

LUCY

Well, thank you very much. I mean grazie.

And wasn't it convenient that one of the few little towns where they still stamped grapes with their feet was right on the outskirts of Rome, near the hotel where Lucy was staying?

So Lucy gets a job at the nearby winery. Lucy said that when she stepped into the vat in her bare feet, it felt like stepping on eyeballs. After a few turns around the vat, she begins to enjoy it until she gets tired and sits on the edge of the vat to rest. The other stamper (played by Teresa Terelli) thinks Lucy is goofing off, bawls her out in Italian, and gives her a little shove causing Lucy to fall. This starts a huge fight, with grape juice flying in all directions. Later, this became one of Lucy's better stories on talk shows. She said the woman didn't speak English (she did), and that they weren't supposed to really fight (they were), and that the woman tried to drown her. Well, let's face it, it's pretty hard to drown in grapes.

In "The Bicycle Trip" where the Ricardos and Mertzes were touring Italy, they were forced to spend the night in a barn. A goat wakes Lucy up by licking her ear. Jerry Miggins, the prop man, said he had to coat Lucy's ear with honey for

Lucy tells Madelyn "You wrote it, you milk it!"

this to work. They were also sharing quarters with a cow, which Lucy eventually milks so they can have something to drink for breakfast. I walked onto the set during rehearsal, and the cow had arrived. It was the saddest, dirtiest-looking cow I had ever seen or maybe cows up close aren't too cute. Lucy gave me a look with those big blue eyes and said, "You wrote it, you milk it!"

One time when he was coming home from Europe, Bob Carroll saw a passenger go through Customs with a large wheel of cheese that he was bringing back from Italy to a friend. Unfortunately, the Customs official thought it looked suspicious and stabbed the cheese with a big knife to see if there were any jewels concealed inside, so the cheese was ruined. This became the basis for the episode where Lucy tries to smuggle in a large cheese in "Home From Europe." Lucy disguises the cheese in a blanket and pretends it's a baby. Her seatmate on the plane was played by Mary Jane Croft, and her character also had a baby wrapped in a blanket. Mary Jane reacted hilariously to Lucy's lack of maternal feelings for the cheese. Years later, Mary Jane told me she always knew when that episode was rerun because people stopped her in the market the next day to tell her all about it.

In 1956, Lucy was nominated for an Emmy again. She had won twice before for best comedian, and this time she was nominated in a rather odd category, "Best Actress in a Continuing Performance," so I guess she thought she wouldn't win because she decided not to attend and asked me to accept for her if the unexpected happened. I didn't have anything to wear, and I didn't have time to shop for a dress, so my husband bought me a dress and I went off to the Emmy Awards, which were held at a dinner at the Pan Pacific Auditorium, and Lucy won. I accepted the award from Art Linkletter, who was the host, and had my picture taken with Lloyd Nolan who was also a winner, and I'm sure he wondered who in the world I was. Later, I ran into Dinah Shore at the Brown Derby, who told me she had seen the show, and she had the same dress, and if she had only known, I could have borrowed hers.

Jess decided to leave the show because his five-year contract with Desilu was up, and he had received an offer to create shows for NBC. He felt a five-year run (153 shows) was enough, that we had done almost every conceivable story line, and we should go off the air while we were still at the top. Desi, on the other hand, thought *I Love Lucy* should go at least one more year. After Jess left, Desi offered the job of producing to Bob and me, but we didn't see how we could write twenty-six shows with Schiller and Weiskopf, oversee production, cast the show, do all the other things Jess did, and sneak in a little personal life since I had been married to Quinn Martin a few months before. It was probably a dumb career move, but we turned it down. But Bob and I did have more to do with the actual running of the show than before. We attended production meetings, discussed sets and casting, and gave notes after rehearsal. We worked closer than before with Desi. We would plot a story line with Schiller and Weiskopf, and then I would go down to the set, where Desi was often in the middle of rehearsal. He would come over to the side and I would ad-lib the story as fast as I could, and he would listen intently. "Fine," he would say, or sometimes, "It's a little soft in the middle," and he was often right. He had excellent powers of concentration and used to drive Lucy crazy by how fast he could memorize his lines. While she was still struggling with hers, he would go run the studio.

I think maybe Desi's greatest contribution to the *Lucy* shows was his enthusiasm. He was never too busy to interrupt whatever he was doing and talk over an idea with us. We would walk down the hall and tell him our latest brainstorm, and he always thought it was great. Or we could ask him if he could get a certain big star who would fit a plot we had, and he would immediately pick up the phone. He never said, "Are you crazy? That will cost too much!" Bob and I have always attributed a great deal of the success of *I Love Lucy* to the fact that Lucy would do absolutely anything we could dream up, and Desi would pay for it. It gave us marvelous creative freedom. Nothing was impossible. If it was funny, we could do it.

I guess we were pretty spoiled. After the various *Lucy* shows were over, Bob and I worked on a series for producer Jimmie Komack's company. We called a meeting of the assistant director and the special effects man to discuss an idea we had to see if they thought it would work. Komack wryly told us that hadn't been a very good idea.

He explained that those people weren't on staff, and he had to pay them for coming to work that day for our meeting. Or as he spelled it out for us, "Desi doesn't own the studio anymore."

The Lucy Gallery

Your Way
HEALTH
VITAMEATAVEGAMIN
FOR HEALTH
3342

Lucy plays the Queen of the Gypsies in "The Operetta."

Lucy wanted real bread as a prop in "Pioneer Women"–and she got it.

Lucy, Ricky, Fred, and Ethel look at the destroyed washing machine in the episode "Never Do Business With Friends."

On their way to California, the gang awakens to find that their motel is next to the train tracks.

When in Switzerland, the Mertzes dress up like the locals.

Lucy learns how to stomp grapes so she can be in an Italian movie.

Lucy, Ethel, and Fred steal John Wayne's footprints.

Trying to replace John Wayne's footprints, Lucy gets her foot stuck in a bucket of cement.

Frank Nelson as the train conductor confronts Lucy in "The Great Train Robbery."

In Paris, Lucy and Ethel are tricked by Ricky and Fred into wearing designer Paris gowns that are actually burlap sacks.

Lou Krugman directs Lucy as a showgirl in Hollywood.

Lucy tries to lead a brood of baby chickens.

Lucy and Harpo Marx.

Lucy and Red Skelton do a number as a couple of tramps in The Lucille Ball-Desi Arnaz Hour.

Desi, Lucy, and Tallulah Bankhead in The Lucille Ball-Desi Arnaz Hour.

Lucy and Milton Berle perform some magic on The Lucy Show.

Lucy and Don Knotts have their first and last blind date on Here's Lucy.

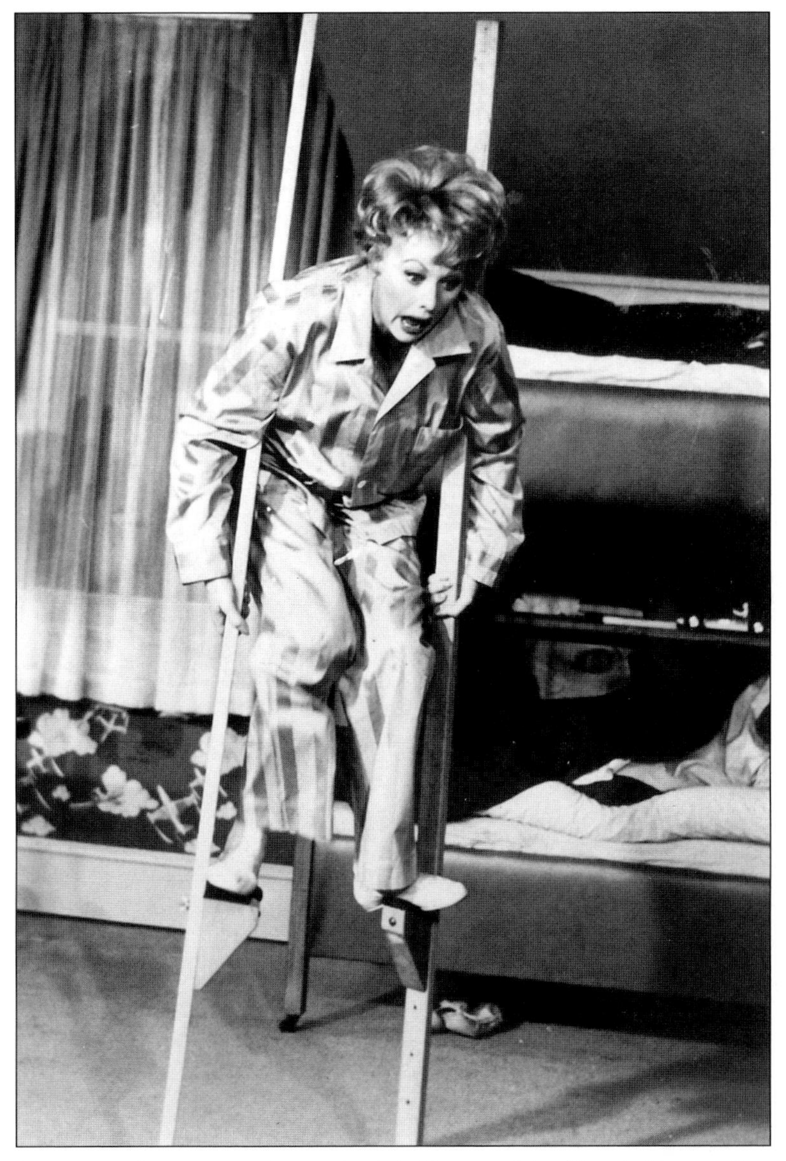

Lucy uses stilts to get to the top bunk in "Lucy and the Electric Mattress" on The Lucy Show.

Like Charlie Chaplin, Lucy was a master of physical comedy—and a comic for the ages.

NINE

Our Longest Laugh

FOR THE SIXTH SEASON, WE DECIDED THAT LITTLE Ricky should be a bit older. The twins who were playing him were very cute, but they weren't old enough to do lines. This is the great advantage to having sitcom children. They can stay in high school for seven years, or they can get three years older during the summer hiatus. Five-year-old Keith Thibodeaux had just appeared on *The Horace Heidt Show*, an NBC variety show, and he was a sensational little drummer. He was hired to portray an older Little Ricky and billed as Richard Keith. His drum playing gave us a lot of story lines: practicing the drums and driving the Mertzes crazy; getting stage fright before the school pageant, and Lucy having to perform with his little combo at the last minute; and Keith and Desi playing the bongo and singing "Babalu" together.

Bob Hope was the guest star on our opening show in an episode cleverly named "Lucy and Bob Hope." Bob and Lucy were old friends and loved working with one another. They swapped TV guest shots and appeared in four movies together. The episode had a baseball theme and in the finale was a number with Lucy, Bob, and Desi, "Nobody Loves the Ump," by Larry Orenstein and Eliot Daniel (Eliot also wrote the *I Love Lucy* theme with Harold Adamson, who wrote the lyrics). Jack Baker was the choreographer. Jack designed most of Hope's dancing numbers, and if you'll notice, they usually involve the same steps, a charming soft shoe. Lucy was not a trained dancer, but she could fake along with anybody, including Van Johnson, Dan Dailey, Shirley MacLaine, Sammy Davis, George Burns, Eddie Albert, Carol Burnett, and Red Skelton. She did the Charleston with Ginger Rogers and Lucie Arnaz, and taught Richard Crenna how to samba.

Orson Welles was also a guest, doing his magic act and levitating Lucy so she seemed to be lying unsupported in space. At one point, Lucy, not knowing she is to be a magician's assistant and thinking she is going to do Shakespeare with Welles, starts reciting Juliet's lines in the balcony scene from *Romeo and Juliet*. Orson Welles answers her, playing Romeo, and I have to tell you the way he did Shakespeare in that incredible, sonorous voice gave you goosebumps even in the middle of a comedy show.

"The Visitor From Italy" was next and was a typical example of how Lucy embraced a physical routine and made it a tour de force. Bob and I were in Hollywood one evening and happened to walk by an Italian restaurant where a man was making pizza in a window. He was throwing the dough up in the air and sort of twirling it around. (I understand they do this to get air in it, but I am certainly not a pizza-making expert. Do not try this at home.) We looked at each other,

Lucy has a visitor from Italy and has to take a job making pizza.

called Lucy, she joined us, and it wasn't long before she was in the window wildly throwing pizza dough about, much to the enjoyment of the crowd that soon gathered outside. The pizza routine was an example of how we sometimes worked. We would think of a funny physical routine for Lucy to do and then work backwards, coming up with a story line so this could be the last big scene. Jay Novello was the fine comedy actor who played Mario, the gondolier from Venice, who knocks on their apartment door one day and announces that he has come to visit them like they said. You know, the old "If you're ever in New York, look us up" kind of invitation. Lucy helps him get a job in a pizza parlor, and then finds out it is against the law for him to work since he is in this country on a visitor's visa, and she has to fill in so he won't lose his back pay. On the show, of course, she was a master of ineptitude, even throwing the pizza up in the air and letting it drop over her head, and then making two little holes in it for her eyes.

We took the Ricardos and Mertzes to Florida for a vacation in an episode called "Deep Sea Fishing," better known to Desi as "Dipsy Fishin'." While there, the two couples make a bet about who can catch the bigger fish, the men or the women, and there was an important bit of business which involved two large identical dead tunas. The foursome had been rehearsing with rubber tunas, which they had to drag back and forth, hiding them from each other in various hotel bathrooms (don't ask). Desi, like Lucy, was very particular about props looking authentic and was a deep-sea fisherman himself, and he thought the tunas looked fake. By the time of dress rehearsal the day before we were to film the show, he was still unhappy. He announced to our assistant director Jack Aldworth that we simply had to have real tunas by the next night. Jack turned pale, but asked, "Can I start looking now, boss?" Desi told him to go. Jack spent half the night calling around hunting for identical tunas, found them at Fisherman's Wharf in San Francisco, had them packed in ice and shipped to the studio. The tunas now looked authentic. Smelly, but authentic.

In that show, we did a scene where our foursome and Little Ricky are deep-sea fishing from a boat. The week before, Bob and I had a moment of giddy power. Desi was fishing off Baja, California, and couldn't be reached. Argyle Nelson, vice president of Desilu Productions, was on vacation, and since Bob and I were at the studio writing and the only ones available, we gave the okay to dig up the nice, smooth floor of the stage and install a huge tank of water so the scene could be filmed in front of the audience. During that scene, Lucy's line gets hooked onto Ricky and, thinking she has a big fish, she pulls Ricky into the water on the other side of the boat.

The Ricardos and The Mertzes go to Florida and try to win a bet over who can catch the largest tuna.

One day at rehearsal, Lucy said to the writers, "Poor Desi has to get in all that dirty water." We knew her well enough that we translated it to mean, "And I sure wish I could get in all that dirty water, too."

Lucy was getting awfully tired of that tiny apartment set and remarked one day maybe the Ricardos should move. We liked the idea. It was logical for them to move to the suburbs since Little Ricky was now of school age, and it gave us a good opportunity for stories about their buying a house, missing the Mertzes, meeting new neighbors, and getting involved in local affairs. We selected Westport, Connecticut, because Bob Weiskopf had lived there and could be our resident expert.

Ralph Berger, the art director, and Claudio Guzman, the set decorator, came up with a beautiful suburban home. The large living room had a big fireplace, an open stairway to a second story, and a charming, spacious entryway. Everyone was thrilled with the larger living room, but after a couple of shows, we found we had a problem. When characters came in the front door and into that spacious entryway, they couldn't say anything important because they weren't in the same room with the people in the living room. So they had to have some unimportant dialogue to cover their entrance. The problem was solved by putting in a Dutch door, which opened immediately into the living-dining room area, and the Mertzes usually made their entrances from there. The lovely open stairway also turned out to be a mixed blessing. If someone made a cutting remark and stalked off to bed, they had to go up a long flight of stairs, which kind of puts a damper on your stalking. We all know that most houses aren't built like TV living rooms with the front door opening right into the room without any hall, but there's a reason why they're constructed that way. If they aren't, a character ends up saying things like, "Don't get up, I'll see myself out."

Another structural oddity is that in sitcoms, closets are almost right by the front door. You never know when you are going to want to have someone huff out the front door and huff into the closet by mistake, or maybe a character is going to leave and opens the door, then says, "Oh oh! He's coming up the walk. I'll hide in the closet until he's gone." Whenever Bob and I looked at the blueprint of a new living room set, we always said, "There has to be a closet by the front door just in case we need it." Never mind that if there is no entry hall, the back of the closet would stick out on the outside of the house like a giant wart. We were doing comedy, not *Architectural Digest*.

Someone once asked us why we did so many shows about people hiding from each other. Well, hiding is as old as French farce. You know. "My husband is coming home! Quick, hide under the bed!" I guess we did do a lot of hiding. Lucy and Ricky hid in the closet in "Sentimental Anniversary." Five guests were hidden in the closet in "Lucy Thinks Ricky Has Been Drafted." Ann Sothern and Lucy hid in the utility closet aboard ship in "Lucy Takes a Cruise to Havana." Lucy hid under a slipcover, in a bass fiddle case, in a steamer trunk, and under a table at least twice. She hid from Harpo Marx in "Lucy and Harpo," and she hid under a serving cart in Cornel Wilde's hotel room in "The Star Upstairs." In "Milton Berle Hides Out at the Ricardos," Milton hid in the den most of the show, and in "Lucy Misses the Mertzes," Ricky, Lucy, Fred, and Ethel all hid in the closet because they thought they heard burglars. I think we finally topped ourselves later when we wrote *The Mothers-in-Law.* We had the four parents come in singly to snoop in their kids' new apartment, then hear someone coming, and hide one by one in a large armoire, which was then tipped on its side and carried out of the room by moving men.

Bob and I cared a lot about our scripts. You would think we were writing *War and Peace*. But we weren't the types to get in a shouting match in defense of our material. When lines were cut that we really liked, Bob used to think in French and pretend he was in Paris, and I doodled on the margins and drew a little, sad, crying face.

We used to write all the comedy business in detail and sometimes Bob drew little blueprints of the scene, like when the Ricardos and all their furniture move in with the Mertzes in "Lucy Hates to Leave." It helped us with the writing and we showed them to the set designer so he would know what nutty business we had in mind. I was very disappointed when things were changed a lot. I complained to Bob in private, and he kept telling me to hold my nose. He even gave me a gold-plated clothespin with the inscription, "If you can't hold your own nose, whose can you hold?"

After they moved to Connecticut, Ricky complains about how high expenses are in their new country home, and Lucy suggests they raise something on their two acres to make extra money. So they decide to raise chickens. This leads to the fact that Fred used to live on a farm and knows all about chickens, so Fred and Ethel relocate to live in the Ricardos' guest house. This became an episode "Lucy Raises Chickens." The subplot was that Lucy and Ricky are going to do a tango for a PTA show at Little Ricky's school.

When we filmed the episode, we found out that baby chickens are a noisy bunch. They never stop cheeping, so they had to be kept outside the stage until their big scene. Then, when they were supposed to follow Lucy across the living room, some of them didn't take directions well and escaped into other parts of the stage and scurried under moving cameras and boom mikes, and the prop men had to move fast to keep it from becoming "The Baby Chicken Massacre."

The Ricardos and Mertzes are planning to split the profits when the chickens start laying eggs, only the chickens don't cooperate and the whole enterprise is becoming a disaster. Ricky and Fred are mad at each other and blaming one another for the financial fiasco and planning to sell off the chickens. Little Ricky and a little pal hear about it and hide some of the chickens at the Mertzes.

Ricky discovers them and calls Fred a "chicken thief." This leads to one of my favorite lines:

ETHEL

If there's one thing Fred isn't, and there's only one thing Fred isn't, it's a chicken thief.

Lucy and Ethel figure it's only a matter of time until the chickens will start to produce. So that the Mertzes won't have to move back to town, the girls buy five cartons of

Lucy does the tango with Ricky, smashes eggs in her blouse, and gets the longest laugh I Love Lucy *ever received.*

eggs and plan to plant them in the nests until the chickens get in the mood. Ricky is about to discover their ruse, so Lucy has to frantically hide as many eggs as possible in her blouse. (There's that hiding again.) Ricky picks this moment to want to rehearse the tango number. We have seen from an earlier rehearsal that the big finish of the number is when Ricky throws Lucy away from him and then brings her back, crushing her to him. Lucy can't talk him out of the rehearsal, and the inevitable happens with Lucy smashing dozens of raw eggs in her blouse. There was a huge laugh, and Lucy's expression was priceless, and just when the laugh started to die down a little, she did that marvelous facial expression and gestures with her hands that said, "I haven't any idea why people are upset, doesn't everyone have raw eggs running down their pants?" It was the longest laugh ever recorded on *I Love Lucy*—65 seconds.

Ethel is trying to figure out how to get out of the room and escape Ricky's wrath when Fred comes from the kitchen and smacks the swinging door into Ethel's back side, where her pockets are filled with eggs, and the laughs started up all over again.

After six years of the show, Desi decided it was time to move on and do something different. After much discussion and negotiations with sponsors and CBS, it was decided that there would be *Desilu Playhouse,* a series of hour shows, interspersed with Desi-Lucy Hours (some called *The Lucy-Desi Comedy Hour* and some called *The Lucille Ball-Desi Arnaz Show*), a 60-minute version of *I Love Lucy.* Bert Granet came aboard as producer.

The writers took a brief vacation and then started in on the first hour show. Desi and Lucy usually spent the month of August at their beach house in Del Mar, California. It was a great vacation for their kids, Lucie and Desi Jr., and was very close to the racetrack, which was one of Desi's hobbies. Lucy didn't mind going to the races, but she was the kind of gambler who would bet two dollars on every horse in the race, and when they crossed the finish line, she would hold up the winning ticket and say proudly, "I had it!" After we finished the script, we planned to have a production meeting to go over the physical aspects of the show. Desi would often hold these early meetings in Del Mar. This meant that the key people had to ride in a studio bus an hour and a half, have the meeting and a quick lunch, and then ride an hour and a half back, and they were less than thrilled.

I had been married for several years to Quinn Martin, who produced *The Untouchables* for Desilu and later headed his own company, Q.M. Productions, which did *The Fugitive, Barnaby Jones, Cannon, The F.B.I.,* and *Streets of San Francisco.* This particular August when Desi summoned the troops to Del Mar, I was five months pregnant. I told my doctor of the impending trip and he wasn't too pleased. I was thirty-six years old and having my first child, and he wanted me to stay close by in case there were complications. I told Desi what the doctor said about my making the trip and he was concerned. He immediately changed plans. "Then I'll come up to Los Angeles and have the meeting there," he said, and he did. I won't say the rest of the staff carried me around the studio on their shoulders, but it was close.

There were thirteen of these specials over three years. The first one was titled "Lucy Takes a Cruise to Havana," written by Schiller, Weiskopf, Bob, and me and directed by Jerry Thorpe, who had started out with us as an assistant director. Incidentally, Jerry's assistant was Jay Sandrich, who later became director of *The Mary Tyler Moore* and *The Cosby Show.* It was to be a flashback kind of show with Lucy telling Hedda Hopper, the Hollywood columnist, how she and Ricky first met. Our guest stars were Ann Sothern, Cesar Romero, and Rudy Vallee.

It was decided to have Danny Cahn, our editor, go to Havana and shoot some film that would match what we did on the stage. Danny flew to Cuba carrying suitcases with matching wardrobes for the doubles he was going to use. He hired a Cuban cameraman and shot a cruise ship landing in the harbor and a horse-drawn carriage in which Lucy, Ricky, Ann Sothern, and Cesar Romero were taking a romantic ride. Danny hired stand-ins for the four and also a stand-in horse for the one we were using on the stage. The horse was called Viejo Pinture (Old Paint) because he was a spotted horse. Danny had trouble finding a double and so they painted the horse to look like the original. Danny told me he was staying at the Hotel Nationale. He said he heard some kind of rumor that Castro and his forces were hiding in the hills and setting off explosions in various buildings. The hotel was supposed to be on the list, so Danny moved. He said he called Desi and told him what kind of footage he was getting, and happened to mention the Castro situation. Desi, who had some experience in revolutions, told him, "Get the hell out of there." Danny came home.

None of us had ever written an hour-long comedy before, so we didn't skimp, and filled it with musical numbers and the film Danny had shot in Havana. When the show was edited, it ran an hour and fifteen minutes. The only thing to cut were the musical numbers, and Desi wasn't about to do that. So he got on the phone and called CBS and the ad agency, J. Walter Thompson, which planned to introduce its client's line of new Ford cars on the show. Desi suggested we "borrow" fifteen minutes from *The U.S. Steel Hour,* a dramatic show that followed us. Of course they said, "You can't do that" and Desi said, "Why not?" and they said, "It's never been done" and Desi said, "Why not?" He casually mentioned that *The U.S. Steel Hour,* whose ratings were not so hot, might benefit from the lead-in. They did and got their highest ratings ever, and to my knowledge it's the only one-hour-and-fifteen-minute show ever done on television. Later, when the show went into syndication, it was cut to an hour, mostly losing the first and last scenes with Hedda Hopper.

A few years ago, the Museum of Television and Radio ran the original hour-and-fifteen-minute show (including the old commercials), which hadn't been seen for more than forty years. Bob and I were on the panel for discussion after the screening. I hadn't seen the show since we filmed it, and I was pleasantly surprised at how well it held up, especially the musical number where Lucy and Ricky realize they are falling in love. It made me feel a little teary because their real feelings for each other came through. The jazzy new Ford cars for 1958, however, seemed just a teensy bit dated.

On the panel with us that night was Arthur Hamilton, who did the lyrics and music for the "Havana" show. Arthur reminded me that when he was working on the numbers, he thought he could use Desi's pronunciation of words as part of the lyrics, so he asked us to send him some examples. Amazingly, he still had the letter I wrote to him about it:

August 23, 1956

Dear Arthur:

Here are as many of Desi's expressions as I could recall:

Desi drops his "ex" prefixes. He says:

'splain for explain; 'zaggerate for exaggerate; 'spensive for expensive

He has trouble with "o" sounds—he says:

hat for hot; Hohney for honey; dunt for don't; wunt for won't

He doesn't seem to like to say two consonants together. He says:

parmen for apartment; mushin pictures for motion pictures; awar for award

He mixes J's and Y's. He calls the musician in his band

Joe Yukl "Joe Jukel." He says yob for job.

He mixes up "t" and "d" sounds. He says:
ret for red; het for head
So Lucy becomes his favorite ret-het.

You really need a second person to point out what he has just said like:

Ricky: That dress is too 'spensive.

Lucy: It is NOT 'spensive.

Ricky: And never mind muckin' my English.

Lucy: I'm not muckin' your English.

If you are seriously thinking of using these, it might be a good idea for you to meet and talk to him. Just tell him that Rubert and Mallen thought you might find somethin' new.

Good luck on the songs.

Sincerely,

Mallen

Arthur told us of a comment Desi made to him during the recording session. Desi said, "You know me, parner, I'm no singer. As a matter of fact, I'm not a very good actor. I can't dance, and I don't write. I don't do anything. But one thing I can do. I can pick people."

During the filming of the "Havana" show, Lucy came to me in the bleachers where I was watching rehearsal and had a little conference with me about a problem she was having. This was something she did from time to time. I don't know why she didn't talk to the director. In the show, Lucy and her pal, Ann Sothern, got into trouble while visiting Havana and were mistakenly put in jail. It was warm, and they were thirsty, so they kept drinking from a nearby water cooler. What they didn't know was that a prisoner who had been picked up for drunkenness had poured a bottle of rum into the water cooler to hide the evidence. They kept drinking and getting a little more tipsy as they waited for someone to come and bail them out. Both were wearing hats and smart little dresses, which is what a tourist would wear in those days. The tipsier Ann got, the more her hat would slip down over one eye, especially when they almost missed the cruise ship and at the last minute were lowered onto the deck on top of a bunch of bananas. Lucy's problem was this. She explained, "You've got to tell Ann Sothern to get rid of that awful hat." I guess I said okay.

Now, I knew perfectly well what the trouble was. Lucy was miffed because somehow Ann had managed to be wearing the funniest hat. I had no idea how to handle this. There was no way I could go to Ann and tell her to get rid of that hilarious hat because Ann, pretty good at comedy herself, would know immediately the source of the problem. I was afraid Lucy's next question to me would be, "Well, did you tell her?" I stalled and did nothing, and it never came up again.

Our second Lucy-Desi Hour starred Tallulah Bankhead, the famous and sometimes infamous stage actress. It was called "The Celebrity Next Door." Tallulah had moved into the house next to the Ricardos in Connecticut, and when Lucy and Ethel found out, they were in a complete state of hysteria. Richard Deacon, the very funny character actor probably best known as "Mel Cooley" on *The Dick Van Dyke Show,* played her butler.

Tallulah had a very deep voice and a great raucous laugh and called everyone in the world "dahling." We met to read the script in Desi's office and things went well, with laughs where they should be. Deacon's character didn't appear until scene four, and when he spoke his first line, Tallulah, who was sitting next to him, roared her famous laugh and said,

"Dahling, you're an actor! I thought you were one of the writers. That's why I was being so nice to you!"

It was when we went on the set to begin rehearsal that the first hint of trouble began. Tallulah couldn't seem to remember her lines or where she was supposed to be on the set. This went on for three days and by dress rehearsal, she was still turning to the script girl Adell Sliff, saying, "What's my line again, dahling?" Lucy, who liked to rehearse and rehearse until it got better and better, was beginning to look tense, and Desi's eyes were starting to bug out. There was a rumor that Miss Bankhead liked to have an alcoholic beverage from time to time, and people were beginning to wonder if the lady from Alabama had some mint juleps stashed in her dressing room.

We always had a note session in Desi's office after rehearsal where the actors, director, and writers discussed any problems. The next day was camera rehearsal, then dinner, and we did the show in front of an audience. We all assembled in Desi's office for notes, and the big topic was going to be "What are we going to do about Tallulah?" Guest stars weren't invited to this particular session. We all took our seats and just as we were about to start, in came Tallulah, saying brightly, "You didn't invite me, but I'm coming anyway." To fill the stunned pause, Lucy remarked, "That's a beautiful sweater." Tallulah had changed from her rehearsal clothes and was wearing slacks and a blouse with a cardigan sweater that had fake pearls and gold beads down the front, a style that was popular at the time. "You like it, dahling, you can have it," she said and took it off and tossed it into Lucy's lap. Vivian cracked, "I'm glad you didn't admire her slacks," and at that point, Tallulah announced, "You can have those, too," and unzipped her pants and let them fall to the floor. I have blacked out on what happened next. I do remember that to everyone's relief, Tallulah was wearing lace-edged panties, and I think Desi said we didn't need to have a note session after all.

The next morning, Desi called Tallulah's agent. I wasn't there, but I understand certain threats were made and "better be sober" was more or less the central theme. That night, in front of the audience, Tallulah was flawless. She remembered every line and belted out every joke. She almost threw the unflappable Miss Ball, who hadn't had a decent rehearsal all week. We never knew if her agent had talked to her or if she was saving it all for the performance, or if she knew all along she was bugging Lucy and was putting us on.

After the show, everyone was milling about on the set, congratulating each other and, of course, all was forgiven because things had turned out so well. I went over to where Tallulah was holding court to thank her for her fine performance. I was seven months pregnant at the time, and she asked me if I wanted a boy or a girl. I told her I really didn't care. "I'll spit on you for luck and make it a boy," she said and actually spit on me. It worked, of course, because my son, Michael Quinn Martin, arrived two months later.

Other hour shows we did that season were "Lucy Hunts Uranium" with the very charming and funny Fred MacMurray; "Lucy Goes to Sun Valley," starring Fernando Lamas; and "Lucy Wins a Racehorse" with Betty Grable and her husband Harry James. In this one, that long staircase in the living room paid off. Little Ricky wants a horse, and Ricky won't get him one because it costs so much to keep. Lucy enters a contest against Ricky's wishes and wins the horse. She has to hide the horse from Ricky—and where else would Lucy hide a horse—in the upstairs guest room. We had a remarkable trained horse who would do almost anything, and he even went halfway up the stairs before Ricky discovered him.

During rehearsal, the writers were called to the set, and we figured, "Oh oh, something's wrong with the script" (writers tend to be a little paranoid, mostly because when they get called to the set, it is hardly ever because the cast is giving a surprise party for them with a big cake that says "Your script is perfect"). So we wondered what needed fixing. When we walked in, the horse was actually sitting quietly in a chair. Lucy couldn't wait for us to see it.

After the first year of the Lucy-Desi Hours, Bob and I decided to retire for a while. I wanted to stay home and be a mom, and Bob wanted to go live in Italy. He dawdled around with his relocation plans and finally left for Rome. About six months after we quit—they had already filmed an hour show with guest star Maurice Chevalier for the next season—I got a call from Desi asking if I would come in and see him. I went to his office, and he drew a chair up beside the desk. We chatted awhile, and he finally got around to the reason for the visit. He was hoping that Bob and I would come back as script consultants and work with Schiller and Weiskopf. He explained that we would only do four shows a season, so there would be time off between and not the grind of weekly run-throughs and rehearsals and writing all weekend so I could be home a lot. He also offered to put in a nursery for my son. I have no memory of why I didn't go for the idea of a nursery, which may have been the first daycare center in the entertainment business, but I did like the idea of working part-time. Besides, my marriage was breaking up, and I wanted to work again. Desi said he would pay to fly Bob home from Italy to talk about it, and if he didn't like the idea, he would pay to fly him back. It all sounded pretty attractive. Desi knew it would, or as he explained to me, "You know what I'm doing, don't you? I'm conning you." It was a perfect example of the Cuban Arm. But it worked. How Desi knew that my marriage was breaking up or that it was raining in Rome and Bob didn't like his new apartment, I'll never know. Maybe it was a lucky Cuban hunch.

In the next two seasons, we did shows with guest stars Red Skelton, Danny Thomas, Ida Lupino and Howard Duff, Milton Berle, Bob Cummings, Ernie Kovacs, and Paul Douglas. The Douglas one was titled "Lucy Wants a Career," and in it Lucy is sick of being a stay-at-home mom and wants to have a job. She becomes a "Girl Friday" on Paul Douglas's morning TV show. She gets stage fright on her first appearance and makes a shambles of the show and is fired. But the audience loves her because she's so natural, and the sponsor tells Paul Douglas he has to hire her back. She likes having a career, but she finds it keeps her from spending time with her son so she quits. I wonder where that idea came from.

In "Lucy Goes to Alaska," she and Red Skelton played a couple of bums and did a song which included a pantomime sketch. I think it was the only time these two superb comics ever did pantomime together, and it was a rare treat.

Bob Cummings was the guest star on "The Ricardos Go to Japan" in which Lucy played a geisha girl. I remember the first day of rehearsal when we were gathered around the table to read the script, Cummings put his closed script on the table and folded his hands. He had already memorized his part. Lucy said, "Show off!" but she loved it because she was a great admirer of someone who came to the set prepared.

Danny Thomas was the star of one of the hour specials, appearing as the character Danny Williams from his own show, along with Marjorie Lord, who played his wife, and his kids, played by Rusty Hamer and Angela Cartwright. The two casts worked really well together. The plot involved Danny renting the Ricardos' house while Ricky made a movie in Hollywood. Only the movie fell through, and because the Williams had a lease, the Ricardos had to move in with the Mertzes. The three couples get into a big wrangle and ended up in court, all suing each other. In the courtroom, the judge was played by Gale Gordon. Due to other commitments, Gale had only appeared twice on *I Love Lucy*, playing Alan Littlefield, Ricky's boss, the owner of the Tropicana Nightclub, and had worked mostly with Desi, so Lucy really hadn't had a big comedy scene with him. She has laryngitis and has to explain to the judge how the Ricardos, Mertzes, Kathy Williams, and Danny (or Banana Nose, as Fred calls him) ended up in such a legal tangle. Lucy acts out the problem in pantomime, and Gale tries to interpret and it showed how beautifully they complemented each other. From then on, Lucy worked with Gale whenever she could. He played the banker Mr. Mooney, who is in charge of her funds, in *The Lucy Show* and her brother-in-law Harry, who was her boss in *Here's Lucy*.

In the hour specials, if we didn't go on location and filmed the whole show in the studio, we used two stages, and during intermission, the audience went outside where soft drinks and sandwiches were served and then went to the adjoining stage. Desi was waiting all day for an important phone call during one of these intermissions. Lucy later said, "How do you like that! While the audience was out having cold cuts, Desi bought RKO!" One reason she was so excited was because she had filmed more than thirty movies for RKO Studios, and now she and Desi owned it.

TEN

The Mertzes

Or As Desi Called Them, "The Merzes"

BOB AND I HAVE ALWAYS FELT THAT ONE OF THE reasons for the success of *I Love Lucy* was the fact that the four principals shared an absolute belief in the material we gave them. No matter what crazy and improbable situations we put them in, they all acted as if it were the most logical thing in the world, which, of course, is what makes it funny. To begin with, Lucy and Desi really loved each other, so we accepted that Lucy and Ricky felt the same way. And let's face it, Vivian and Bill just WERE the Mertzes. Lucy and Vivian had great chemistry as friends, and Frawley was perfect as the curmudgeon with a heart of gold (who comes in, has two lines, and gets a big laugh). As writers, it would be nice to talk about "shaping the characters" and "tailoring the material," but it would be more truthful to admit that sometimes you're lucky, and great performers just fall into your lap.

After Vivian and Bill were hired, we were delighted to learn that both could sing very well and dance. Vivian had been in musicals on Broadway, and when Bill was in vaudeville, he introduced the old standards "Melancholy Baby" and "Carolina in the Morning." We had them do a version of this last number in "Ricky Loses His Voice." Whenever the script called for a musical number for the two, Viv usually choreographed it and insisted on Bill rehearsing with her, much to his disgust. But he forgave her when they got a big hand from the audience.

Vivian liked to say that it was in her contract that she had to weigh twenty pounds more than Lucy so she would look like a dumpy, frowsy housewife. I never saw her contract, but I think this was just something she liked to say in case she got into the cookies too often. If you look at some of the early shows where Vivian is wearing those tight-waisted dresses with big skirts that were popular in the '50s, you can see she has a rather tiny waist. She was such a fine comedian and such a great foil for Lucy, we didn't care what she weighed. Mary Wickes, a fine comedy actor herself, said, "Vivian Vance is the best second banana in the business," and coming from Mary, that was a real compliment.

When we first started doing the show, we learned that Bill used to tear his scenes out of the script, and they were the only ones he paid attention to. When he wasn't in a scene, he would go to his dressing room, so sometimes he was a little vague on what the show was about. This is the way he was used to doing it in the movies. He was never the lead, so he would be hired for a few weeks, learn his lines, do his scenes, get paid, and go home. Of course, he would hear our script being read for the first time around the table, but more than once, I noticed him nodding off. The only trouble was, sometimes a gag would be planted in the first scene, maybe played on in the second scene, and when

Ethel tells Fred about Lucy's latest scheme.

Fred Mertz entered in the third scene, he would have the same line and get a huge laugh and have no idea why. After a few times, he started paying attention to the whole script. I have no idea of his background, and I never knew anything about his childhood, but obviously no one read to him as a child because in a script we had someone call someone else "Chicken Little" and make a joke about the sky falling. Bill asked crossly, "Who the hell is Chicken Little?"

The Fred Mertz character was a combination of my Uncle Oscar, who was pretty tight with a buck, and Bob's Uncle Bert. "For corn sake!" was one of Uncle Bert's favorite expressions, and "Good night, nurse!" was from Uncle Oscar. We could dress Bill up in anything—a toga, a night shirt and night cap, a top hat and a monocle, kilts and a tam. When he entered the room, it was a guaranteed laugh.

A lot of the words and expressions we used in the show were taken from Bob's and my relatives. Fred's "What the Sam Hill!" was from my father. When Tennessee Ernie Ford was our guest star, Lucy was doing her sexy walk to "vamp" him and scare him into going back home. Ernie watched her and remarked that "You've got quite a hitch in your get-along," which was from Bob's father.

We borrowed a word Bob's mother used when she was describing a drab color in "The Ballet" episode. Ethel asks Lucy a personal question:

ETHEL

I've always wondered. Lucy, what color is your hair really?

LUCY

I don't know what you're talking about. My hair is red.

ETHEL

Well, let me put it this way—what color are your roots?

LUCY

Guess.

ETHEL

Blonde?

LUCY

No.

ETHEL

Black?

FRED

Green?

LUCY GIVES HIM A LOOK.

LUCY

No. It's uh—how do you like that? It's been so long, even I can't remember.

SHE GOES TO THE MIRROR AND LOOKS AT THE PART IN HER HAIR.

LUCY (CONT'D)

Oh, of course. It's muckle-de-dun.

ETHEL

Muckle-de-what?

LUCY

Muckle-de-dun. That was my grandmother's word for tan that didn't have the guts to be brown.

After writing a first draft of this book, I asked Tom Watson to read it for errors. Tom is president of Lucy's fan club, and he knows more about the Lucy shows than I will ever remember. He caught quite a few bloopers, and when he came to the above exchange, he said, "I have to tell you something, that wasn't in the show." I couldn't believe it since I had copied the dialogue out of my bound copy of the script. So I ran the video and sure enough, the discussion of Lucy's hair in the opening of the show was cut. I'm sure Lucy didn't cut it because she was sensitive about not being a natural redhead. We did a lot of jokes about her hair being dyed, and she loved them, so it was probably cut for time.

I don't remember how we came up with the names Fred and Ethel, but I remember where Mertz came from. Naming characters for a comedy series is hard. You want a sort of unusual name, but not a name that sounds like you're trying

Vivian Vance, Desi Arnaz, Bill Frawley, and Lucille Ball celebrate winning Best Situation Comedy and Vivian's win for Best Supporting Actress at the Emmy Awards on February 11, 1954.

too hard to be funny, and you want a name that you think is right because you will have to live with it forever if you're lucky and the show is successful. I remembered a family who lived down the street from me in Indianapolis when I was a kid—a Dr. and Mrs. Mertz and their two sons Jack and Dick. Bob liked the name, so we made them Ethel and Fred Mertz. I had no idea, of course, that our Mertzes would become so well-known, or I might have been more hesitant. Some years later, I was at the Indiana University-Southern California Rose Bowl football game when someone tapped me on the shoulder. It was Jack Mertz, now a doctor, and he was sitting behind me. This was not as much of a coincidence as it sounds because this was the only time Indiana's football team had ever won the Big Ten Championship and come to the Rose Bowl, so just about the entire population of the state of Indiana was in the stands. I told Jack I had dreaded ever running into him because I thought his family was probably furious with me. He assured me that they all loved it and were enjoying the publicity.

A few years ago, I received a letter from Dr. Susan Mertz Ivancevich of Indianapolis. She explained that her grandmother was an accomplished artist and was having a show and they thought it would be fun if I would write a letter for display, explaining how we named our characters after her and her husband. She told me her grandmother's full name, which I never knew, and it was Ida Ethel Mertz! Kind of spooky, huh?

We sometimes named characters after our friends or Lucy's friends. They got a kick out of it, and it saved a lot of time. In "The Operetta," for which Bob and I wrote the lyrics (okay, so they weren't very good, but they weren't supposed to be since Lucy wrote them herself), Ricky sang a song, "The Good Prince Lancelot" to Vivian, who was playing the character Lily of the Valley:

"I am the good Prince Lancelot,
I like to sing and dance a lot.
I have an eye for a pretty face.
I like the girls and it's no disgrace.
There was Mercedes, Rosalind, Betty and Sue,
There was Dorothy, Janis and sweet Mary Lou,
Audrey, Vivian, and Estelle
But that's all over with now."

Lancelot's girlfriends were named for Bob's sisters, my sisters, Jess' wife and his secretary. Other names of friends of Bob's and mine who appeared in the show were Judge Paul Roney, Marge and Chuck Van Tassel, Howdy Wilcox, and Betty Jo Hanson. The owner of the pizza place where Lucy tossed pizza in the front window just happened to be Tony DiBello, our secretary Elaine's father.

Bob and Madelyn at the piano work on the lyrics for "The Operetta."

I would like to explain that in "Pregnant Women," when Lucy considers naming the baby "Little Madelyn" or "Little Robert," we didn't write this. Lucy added it on the set as a gag. Another thing added on the set was in "Lucy's Last Birthday," when a contortionist act was named "Pugh and Carroll."

Lucy liked to work with actors she knew, and many of the actors who appeared on her shows were those she had worked with in radio. Radio actors were also great for a show that was shot in front of an audience because their training is to learn things quickly and get it right. There were no retakes in radio. One who appeared often was Mary Jane Croft. Her first role on *I Love Lucy* was as Cynthia Harcourt, a wealthy former school friend of Lucy's, in "Lucy is Envious." She then portrayed the woman who sat next to Lucy on the plane

Lucy and Mary Jane Croft on the airplane returning from Europe. Mary Jane has a baby, Lucy has a cheese called "Chester."

in "Return From Europe" when Lucy is smuggling home a large cheese. She was also "Betty Ramsey," the next-door neighbor, in five different episodes when the Ricardos moved to Connecticut, and she played "Audrey Simmons" during the early years of *The Lucy Show*. She later was Mary Jane on *Here's Lucy*.

Another actor who worked a lot on the show was Frank Nelson. Frank had been on Lucy's radio show several times. He worked all the time in radio, often on Jack Benny's show. Frank could be quite outspoken, and there was a time during rehearsal of *My Favorite Husband* when he said something sarcastic that didn't sit so well with Lucy. She took Jess aside and told him, "I don't want that man on my show anymore." After the show was over and Frank got his customary share of huge laughs, Lucy told Jess, "I was wrong. He's too funny. Let's use him." It was typical. She had cooled down and realized she was overreacting, and if you were funny, Lucy would forgive you almost anything. Frank worked on the show

Madelyn and Bob are extras at the sidewalk café in "Paris at Last."

dozens of times in various roles, including Betty Ramsey's husband, Ralph. He was always terribly good, and we were very glad Lucy had a change of heart.

Jerry Hausner appeared on at least eleven shows, and did off-scene baby cries when the baby who played Little Ricky didn't feel like crying on cue. Jerry later said he learned how to do baby cries years before when he was in vaudeville from Pepito the Clown, who taught Lucy the cello routine for the *I Love Lucy* pilot. Bobby Jellison was the bellboy at the hotel in five of the shows when the Ricardos were in Hollywood.

Shirley Mitchell appeared on the show as Marion Strong, who was named for an old friend of Lucy's from Jamestown, and Doris Singleton often played Carolyn Appleby, who had been one of Lucy's teachers.

Bob Carroll Jr., was an extra in the show three times. He was at the rail standing next to Ethel in "Bon Voyage" and he was wearing a fez and seated at the roulette table in "Lucy Goes to Monte Carlo." He wore a beret at the next table in an outdoor café when Lucy is served escargot in "Paris at Last." If you look closely, when Bob toasts Lucy with his wine glass, there is an elbow in the shot. It belongs to someone who is next to him. Guess who! Lucy asked if we wanted to be extras in the show since Bob fit right in with his French-looking beard, so we agreed, but nobody told the cameraman to include both writers in the shot. You can see the whole me again in the background if you look really fast when Lucy is escorted from the café by gendarmes for passing counterfeit French francs. Bob enjoyed doing it, but I was a wreck. I went home to get something special to wear, I had my makeup done by Lucy's makeup man Hal King, and dithered around all day when I should have been writing. I learned that my place was behind the camera, and my elbow was never nominated for an Emmy.

ELEVEN

What's New?

THE '60S WERE A TURBULENT TIME FOR THIS country, and there were a lot of changes in that decade in my personal life and those around me as well. In the 1960s, I was divorced from Quinn Martin. Lucy and Desi were divorced. Bob Carroll's only daughter Christina was born. Lucy was married to Gary Morton in 1961, and Desi married Edie Hirsch in 1963. Vivian married John Dodds in 1961, and I was married to Dr. Richard Davis, a widower with four children, in 1964. It must have been something in the California water.

I also moved from California to Indiana, lived there for almost two years, and moved back to California again. Bob and I wrote *The Lucy Show* for two seasons, wrote two TV specials, two movies, rewrote another, did a rewrite on a Broadway musical, created three pilots, including one for

Vivian Vance and Lucille Ball arouse the suspicion of Gale Gordon on The Lucy Show.

Carol Channing who was then the star of Broadway's *Hello, Dolly!,* and were head writers on *The Mothers-in-Law* for two years. Not to mention being in the middle of the Bel-Air fire in Los Angeles and a tornado in Indiana. I kept hoping somebody would ask me, "What's new?"

After her divorce, Lucy thought she needed a change of scene, so she accepted a lead in the Broadway musical *Wildcat,* took her children and her mother to New York, and moved into an apartment. The book of the musical was written by Richard Nash, with music by Cy Coleman and lyrics by Carolyn Leigh. Desi was involved in the financing of the show, and he suggested Bob and I write a special for TV that we called *Lucy Goes to Broadway.* It was to be a fictional account of the Lucy character going to New York to try to get a part in a musical. We planned to film it during the day in New York while she was doing the play at night. Notice how we all took it for granted that Lucy could star in a musical at night and film a TV special in the daytime? Incidentally, even though Lucy and Desi were divorced, if I was in Desi's office when she happened to call him, I could always tell he was talking to Lucy by the loving tone of his voice.

Our script opened with Lucy and Vivian Vance (playing themselves, but really playing their TV characters) running into each other at Sardi's Restaurant in New York and discovering they are both up for the lead in a new musical *Wildcat.* Vivian points out that Lucy can't really sing, but Lucy finds this a minor drawback.

VIVIAN

Lucy, I don't mean to be unkind, but there's something you seem to be overlooking. How can you do a musical? You don't know how to sing.

LUCY

(NETTLED) What's that got to do with it?

VIVIAN

Look, I've heard you sing and it has nothing to do with the word "musical." People aren't going to pay good money to hear something like that. It would be easier for them to stay home and run their nails across the blackboard.

Lucy and Vivian both promise to drop out of the competition and let the other one have the role and neither means it. They secretly try to influence Bob Hope, who is in town and one of the backers of the show. Besides Bob Hope, others who were to appear in the show were Bill Frawley, playing himself, Richard Nash, Michael Kidd, the director, the lead actors in the musical, Keith Andes and Paula Stewart, plus Ed Sullivan. Lucy is supposed to audition for the director and makes a frantic attempt to work on her singing voice. She calls her pal Leonard Bernstein, then the conductor of the New York Philharmonic Orchestra, and begs him to help her. She interrupts him in the middle of an orchestra rehearsal and reminds "Lenny" that they both worked at MGM. Bernstein politely points out that they worked at MGM at different times, but since he is short of time and would really like to get rid of her, he gives her a singing lesson in front of the whole orchestra. Lucy gets the part, and Vivian is given the lead in a revival of *Come Back, Little Sheba*. We planned to include some of the numbers from *Wildcat* as a finale.

This time it looked as if Bob and I would really get a big "freebie." Desi planned to give us an all-expense-paid trip to New York, with suites at a top hotel, plus rooms for my son, Michael, our secretary, and my housekeeper. Lucy told us, "You've got to have a limo. You can't get around in New York without a limo." We told Desi that Lucy said we have to have a limo. He made a face and then agreed. But it didn't happen. After a few months in the musical, Lucy, who was in almost every number and who didn't really have a trained voice, became sick and exhausted and had to drop out, and there went our special, our free trip, and our limo.

We did, however, get an all-expense-paid trip on two different weekends to Washington, D.C. Well, actually, it was a working trip. One day Lucy called us to her office to meet Morton DaCosta, who was a pal of hers. He was in rehearsal, directing a musical *Hot Spot,* starring Judy Holliday, Academy Award winner for *Born Yesterday,* and they were in tryouts in Washington, D.C., prior to going to Broadway. Apparently, the show had a lot of problems and Lucy had been singing our praises, because Mr. DaCosta was hoping we could come back and fix the book. As I look back now, I'm not sure why in the world any of us thought Bob and I could improve a Broadway musical. We had no experience writing a musical, as I hardly think you can count doing the lyrics for "The Pleasant Peasant" in "The Operetta" episode of *I Love Lucy* on the same level with Rogers and Hammerstein.

It was arranged that we could work on the TV show during the week and fly to Washington on weekends to bring our magic touch to DaCosta's show. We took the red-eye to Washington and went to the theater. We had a copy of the script, and we asked the stage manager if we could have an updated copy, since changes were being made all the time. "Oh, there isn't one," he replied. We sensed we might be in over our heads.

It went downhill from there. Numbers were put into the show one night and taken out the next. Judy Holliday was seriously ill and trying bravely to carry on. We met the writers, Jack Weinstock and Willie Gilbert, and they had done so many versions of the book that they had them stacked on the floor around the walls of their hotel room. They were thrilled to see any kind of help—even us.

We sat in the audience our first night, and I took notes on a lighted clipboard, feeling terribly important. In the morning, because everyone had given a performance the night before and were sleeping in, we ran around as fast as we could to look at Washington landmarks. On the second weekend we were there, Morton DaCosta's ulcer got out of hand. The talented man summoned us to his hotel room to give us his notes to pass on to the cast, and they took him off to the hospital. We called a meeting with Judy Holliday, the producers, and the cast and gave them his notes and ours. We moved numbers and cut scenes and changed dialogue and in general did a big overhaul. They listened intently. Bob and I flew back to Los Angeles. They hired a new director and didn't do a thing we suggested, and we never saw any of them again.

A few years later, I was on the picket line during a strike

by the Writers Guild and fell into step with Larry Gelbart, who developed the *M*A*S*H* TV series and is an Academy Award-winning movie writer and playwright. Our big adventure with *Hot Spot* came up. "Oh, I went back there to help on that one, too," he said, "practically everybody did."

Shortly after this, Bob saw an article in the paper about a family named Beardsley who lived in Carmel, California. It was a story about Frank, a widower, and Helen, a widow, who had fallen in love and married. What made it so unusual was that Frank had ten children and Helen had eight. We told Desi about it, and he liked it as a movie for Lucy. So we went to Carmel, California, for the weekend, taking my son, our secretary, and my housekeeper. We went to the Beardsley's house and met everyone and asked a lot of questions about just how they handled having eighteen children. They were charming people, and Frank, who was retired from the Navy, said he organized the family as if he were still in the service. I noticed he ran a tight ship, and the children all behaved very well. He explained that when the parents weren't home, the oldest child was the officer in charge.

They had added three bedrooms and two baths to their home when they got married, so there were four children in bunk beds in each room, although the oldest child always had a room to himself. There was a large family room which had bins marked with sizes for laundry. You didn't wear your own socks, you got the right size out of the bin. They had two station wagons for transportation. I asked Frank how they all went out to dinner. He laughed and said, "Oh, we don't go out to dinner." There seemed to be only one TV, and we asked how they decided who watched what. Helen told us that the oldest child in the room got to choose. It was nearing dinner time, and Helen explained that the older boys did the cooking, and she did the desserts. At one point, I looked over and one of the sons was getting ready to broil an entire sink full of chicken. We thought it was time to leave, but Helen invited the five of us to stay for dinner. We said we couldn't impose like that and she said, "What's five more?"

I noticed that the small children seemed to want to sit on the guests' laps a lot, and I sensed that maybe there were times when there weren't enough laps to go around. It was interesting to see my three-year-old Michael's reaction to this. He was puzzled why anybody would want to sit on my lap, which had always been available, and pretty soon he wanted to sit on my lap, too.

Desi bought the rights to the Beardsley's story, and Bob and I wrote a script. The picture was made several years later at United Artists and was called *Yours, Mine and Ours* in reference to the fact that Helen and Frank had two more children together, bringing the total to twenty. The script was eventually rewritten by Mel Shavelson and Mort Lachman, with Bob and I getting a "story by" credit. Lucy starred in it with Henry Fonda, and it was very successful and is still shown on TV today.

On the morning of November 6, 1961, Bob called and asked if I had the TV on. I didn't, and he suggested I might want to check it because there seemed to be a rather large raging fire nearby. I turned on the TV and watched the beginning of one of the worst fires Los Angeles ever had. I lived in a small house at the top of Bel-Air, and the fire was coming across Beverly Glen canyon, which I could see from the back of my house. Bob was renting a house in Beverly Glen and was closely watching the progress of the blaze. It is interesting to me how we now get our information about disasters from TV. I was glued to the set, and it wasn't long before firemen were making the rounds of everyone's homes and telling people they had to get out because the fire was coming up the hill behind. There are lots of stories of what people grab to salvage from burning buildings. Michael was

Producer Elliott Lewis meets with writers Bob Weiskopf, Bob Schiller, Madelyn, and Bob Carroll Jr. on the set of The Lucy Show.

home from preschool with a cold. I went into my "I'm calm and I'm in charge" mode, collecting some of his clothes and favorite toys, my best clothes and jewelry, the baby pictures, artwork, important papers, called grandmothers and friends to tell them we were okay and where we were going, and Michael and I calmly drove away without a stitch of underwear for either one of us.

Desi called from Palm Springs to offer his penthouse at the Chateau Marmont. As I drove along Sunset Boulevard toward his apartment, the entire sky above the hills was reflected red from the fire for miles. Bob's rental house was burned to the ground, and he and I both stayed at Desi's place for several days. I couldn't get back into my house for a week. It was two days before I even knew if I had a house or not. It turned out to be the only house on the small street that didn't burn, possibly because of the rock roof. The front door was scorched and all the shrubbery was black. All in all, the fire burned more than five hundred homes, even jumping the 405 Freeway to burn homes in Brentwood before the firemen finally put it out. Amazingly, no lives were lost. To this day, when I hear a fire engine, I stop and listen to see where it is headed and sometimes go outside to see if I can see smoke anywhere.

In 1962, Lucy decided she would go back into television. Desi found a book called *Life Without George* by Irene Kampen, the story of two single moms, one widowed, one divorced, who pool their resources and live together in Danfield, Connecticut, coping in a life without men and raising their kids. This became *The Lucy Show* starring Lucy as Lucy Carmichael and Vivian Vance as Vivian Bagley. Lucy's children were played by Candy Moore and Jimmy Garrett, and Vivian's son was portrayed by Ralph Hart. I recently ran into all the kids, of course now grown, at a Lucy convention and Ralph showed me a silver dollar we had given him for one of his performances and said he still carried it.

On the new series, Desi was executive producer, Elliott Lewis was the producer, and Jack Donohue was director. Schiller and Weiskopf and Bob and I were the writers. Elliott Lewis was the husband of Mary Jane Croft, who appeared in many of the various Lucy series, and he was a multitalented man. He started out in radio as a prominent actor, later became a TV writer, director, and producer, and wrote five mystery novels. He also worked with us as producer of *The Mothers-in-Law.* He was very calm and professional, and when I became a producer, he taught me one of the most important things—always be sure an actor has a good dressing room.

When he was directing *Petticoat Junction,* one of the crew said to him, "You must be happily married," and Elliott said, "How can you tell?" and the man said, "Because you always get your work done in time to go home to dinner." Elliott apparently had also studied at the Desi Arnaz School of "Why Not?" because I remember we were writing a script for *The Lucy Show* one night and got a crazy idea at one o'clock in the morning and called him. We asked, "If Lucy misses the train, can we have Vivian in the compartment, and the train is moving and she looks out the window and we see Lucy riding by on a horse, trying to catch up?" Elliott said, "Sure," and went back to sleep, and we did it. All in front of an audience.

While *The Lucy Show* did not have the longevity of *I Love Lucy,* it was extremely popular, and Lucy did some really great routines in it. She and Vivian put up a TV antenna, installed a shower, went into the business of giving children's parties, learned judo, and opened a restaurant together. Lucy also took up golf, went into politics, conducted a symphony, and became a process server, a reporter, a referee, and an astronaut.

There was one show called "Lucy is Kangaroo for a Day" in which Lucy needs money to buy her son a bicycle, so she gets a part-time job as a secretary for the wonderful character actor John McGiver. She totally bombs out as a secretary, having only been to secretarial school for a few weeks fifteen years before, and McGiver gives her one more chance before she gets fired. She is to pick up some important papers and deliver them to him where he is having lunch with a client. She picks up the papers, but unfortunately the knit dress she is wearing gets snagged on the elevator and her dress unravels, so she is left standing in her slip. Nearby is a rack of costumes (wasn't it lucky this happened near a costume shop with a rack of Halloween outfits?), but all she can find in her size is a kangaroo suit. She appears in the restaurant, much to the amusement of the other diners. The way Lucy tried to appear unconcerned (doesn't everybody wear a kangaroo outfit to lunch?) was a pure Lucy moment. She even took her own tail and flung it around her neck nonchalantly as if it

Vivian Vance and Lucille Ball in "Lucy and Viv Install a Shower" from The Lucy Show.

were a fur scarf. And who else could do justice to the look of a kangaroo who just spilled hot soup in her own pouch?

In "Lucy and Viv Install a Shower," the actresses showed what really good sports they were. Lucy decides to install a new shower herself because the plumber is too expensive. They are inside the shower when the faucet breaks off, sending a stream of water inside, which quickly fills up the space. The door won't open because Lucy has installed it backwards, so it opens inward, and the pressure of the water keeps it shut. They soon are treading water that was actually over their heads, but they never utter a word of complaint. Lucy, however, did make this one of her better stories on talk shows. The way she told it when she went down under the water to open the drain (all planned), she would have drowned if Vivian hadn't pulled her up by the hair. Well, as Desi used to say, "Lucy 'zaggerates."

I recently reread another episode from that series, "Lucy and Her Electric Mattress," and found one of my disappointed little faces because something got cut. Vivian and her son, Sherman, have been on a trip and arrive home very late, having had car trouble.

The page looked like this:

INT. KITCHEN - NIGHT

THE DOOR OPENS AND VIVIAN AND SHERMAN ENTER. AS VIV TURNS ON THE LIGHTS, WE SEE THAT THEY ARE WEARY AND CARRYING SUITCASES.

SHERMAN
Boy, Mom, I'm sure tired.

VIVIAN
Me, too. I'm sorry my old car wouldn't make it to Uncle Ned's.

SHERMAN
Well, you couldn't help it. It wasn't your fault the transmission dropped out.

VIVIAN
That's true. I didn't even know I had one. I'll tell you one thing—next time we take a trip,

I'll carry a spare transmission in the glove compartment.

SHERMAN

Mom, that won't work, but I'm too tired to explain why.

THEY START UP THE STAIRS.

VIVIAN

I'm too tired to understand. Honestly, when I think of how long it took before a motorist stopped to help us... Who did those other cars think we were—a short hood and his blonde accomplice?

I remember in rehearsal Vivian questioned the dialogue. She thought it wasn't valid. She asked, "Why wouldn't we have had that conversation in the car?" Desi carefully explained, "Because if you had that conversation in the car, the audience wouldn't have heard you."

This was the same show in which Lucy and Viv, through a series of incidents, have to sleep in the top bunk of a two-bunk bed. Their combined weight causes the bed to slowly give way and their expressions as they sink out of sight were classic.

Gale Gordon joined the show in its second year and played the banker Mr. Mooney, who is in charge of Lucy's finances. The chemistry between them was terrific, and one of my favorite episodes was called "Lucy Gets Locked in the Vault," which Bob and I wrote with Bill O'Hallaran. Lucy is trying to talk to Mr. Mooney who is in the vault, and he refuses to talk to her, so she pulls the door shut, not realizing she is locking them together in there for twenty-four hours. Lucy has been shopping and in her bag is some uncooked macaroni, and since they haven't eaten for six hours, they find it rather tasty. She also has a pack of children's playing cards in her bag, so they play poker with the bank's money.

LUCY

I'm opening for five thousand.

SHE PUSHES A STACK OF BILLS ONTO THE TABLE.

MOONEY

I'll see you and raise you twenty thousand.

HE SHOVES A STACK OF BILLS FORWARD.

LUCY

I'll see you and raise you fifty.

SHE SHOVES SOME BILLS FORWARD.

MOONEY

Fifty it is. (HE SHOVES OUT HIS LAST STACK) I'll call you.

LUCY

I hope you know what you're doing.

MOONEY

Oh, I do, all right. Take a look at that. (LAYING DOWN HAND) Three piggies and two bunnies. (HE REACHES FOR THE POT)

LUCY

(RESTRAINING HIM) Just a moment. (SHE SPREADS HER HAND) Four lambs and a billy goat. And remember, billy goats are wild.

We did several shows around the town's all-women Volunteer Fire Department. The volunteers consisted of Lucy, Viv, and some of her other pals, including Fire Fighters Mary Wickes, Mary Jane Croft, and Carole Cook. In one of the episodes, the fire fighters tried to raise money for new fire hoses by putting on a show. They chose *Cleopatra*, and of course Lucy gave herself the title role. Vivian wasn't too pleased about this and complained about her small part, or as she put it, "The asp has more lines than I do!"

TWELVE

Did You Really Try Out All Those Stunts?

When people watch Lucy on the old shows, they probably think, "Look at all that funny stuff she thinks up to do." Well, it's true, she was gifted and hilarious, but in each of the scripts there were large blocks of direction in capital letters, which Lucy used to call THE BLACK STUFF. People may assume that we wrote LUCY COMES INTO THE ROOM WEARING A CRAZY HAT AND DOES SOMETHING FUNNY. Not exactly. Each gag was carefully planned. One reason we wrote everything in such detail was because we were too busy to go to the production meetings (I don't think we were invited, either, but mostly we didn't have the time because we were writing) and we didn't spend a lot of time on the set for the same reason. We wanted it to be perfectly clear what we had in mind. I recently read the script "Lucy Thinks Ricky is Getting Bald" from the first season of *I Love Lucy* and I couldn't believe the direction I had written:

RICKY ENTERS THE KITCHEN. HE IS WEARING A HAT, PULLED DOWN AROUND HIS EARS. NOTE: WE MUST SCREEN THE LIVING ROOM SO THE AUDIENCE DOESN'T SEE HIM UNTIL HE ENTERS THE KITCHEN TO AVOID AN UNEXPLAINED LAUGH LIKE WE HAD LAST WEEK WHEN RICKY HAD LITTLE BANDAGES ON HIS FACE FROM SHAVING IN COLD WATER IN "THE PIONEER WOMEN" SHOW.

After that bossy little instruction, I can't imagine why a member of the crew didn't accidentally drop one of those big heavy 10K lamps on my head. But I wanted to be sure they got it right!

Bob and I always tried out the stunts ourselves whenever possible. We wanted to be sure it worked instead of waiting until we were on the set with fifty people standing around and finding out it couldn't be done. Then, too, by trying it out, we often found funnier things than we had imagined. An example was a gag in "The Handcuffs" episode of *I Love Lucy*. As a joke, Lucy handcuffs herself to Ricky, and then finds out she doesn't have the right key so she can't unlock them. Bob and I handcuffed ourselves together and then tried to get ready for bed, like in the script. We found that if you are handcuffed to another person, you can't get out of your jacket or blouse because the sleeves and the entire coat bunch up around your wrists. So we made that part of the routine.

It was good we tried out another routine before we put it in the script. When Lucy's knit dress unravels in "Kangaroo for a Day," we wrapped me up in string, and Bob pulled the string as if it caught on an elevator. We discovered that if I didn't whirl around, I would ostensibly be sucked down the elevator shaft. So when Lucy got dizzy from whirling, she had to keep leaping up over the string like a jump-rope, so it would keep unwinding. I'll admit it sounds like a pretty silly thing for two grown people to be doing, but that's what we were getting paid for.

When we wrote THE BLACK STUFF in the script, we would then write (WE TRIED THIS) to let the actors know it was feasible. Lucy was sometimes skeptical the first time she read it, and Desi would say, "Honey, they said they tried it, so try it and if you don't like it, they'll write something else." And then, of course, she would do it and improvise on it and almost always like it.

If a stunt was something that Lucy was going to do by herself, I used to try it first because we wanted to see if it was physically possible for a woman to do, and we also wanted to be sure Lucy wouldn't get hurt. It was okay if I got hurt because I was replaceable, but Lucille Ball wasn't. I remember one gag that wasn't a good idea. Lucy was to be tied to a swivel chair and was supposed to glide backward across the room in a scene in *Here's Lucy* where Lucy and Mike Connors, playing his TV role Mannix, are being held hostage by bank robbers. I tried the stunt, and the chair flipped over backwards, giving my head a good whack on the floor. So instead, we had them tied back to back in chairs so they could sort of hop across the room together.

Doing all the research, I got quite an education. I learned how to dip candy, how to crush eggs in my blouse, and how to do judo and karate. In "Someone's On the Ski Lift With Dinah" in *Here's Lucy* with Dinah Shore as a guest star, I learned how to wear skis (that wouldn't come off) and roll over the office coffee table on my back. I learned how to act as if I'd had too many sleeping pills and go totally limp (although nobody could get as limp as Lucy) so that Bob, acting as Paul Douglas in "Lucy Wants a Career," could try to put a coat on me. I found out that walking on stilts wasn't too difficult, although what Lucy did with stilts in "Lucy and Her Electric Mattress" was inspired. I also learned how to ride a unicycle and went smack into a wall, so we decided it was entirely too dangerous a thing for our star to do.

In *The Lucy Show* in an episode called "Loophole in the Lease," Lucy was trying to get out of Vivian's bedroom without being seen, and we wanted Lucy to roll herself up in a rug and roll out of the room. I wasn't too thrilled to be rolled up in a rug with my arms pinned to my side as if I were in a straitjacket, having a slight touch of claustrophobia. I said I would do it only if Bob Carroll would get me out the minute I asked to be unrolled. I had a feeling that Schiller and Weiskopf might think it was pretty funny to leave me rolled up and go to lunch. As a matter of fact, it was a good thing we tried it because, of course, the gag didn't work. You don't roll out the door in a 6'x 8' rug longways, you roll sideways, which makes it impossible to get through the door, and we had to think of something else.

Another routine that didn't work out was a taffy pull that we were going to use in "Tennessee Bound" when the Ricardos and Mertzes were on their way to California and stopped in Bent Fork, Tennessee, to visit their cousin Ernie Ford and his family. They get arrested for speeding while driving through the tiny town. In order to get them out of jail, Ernie promises to marry one of the Sheriff's twin daughters Teensie and Weensie, played by Rosalyn and Marilyn Borden. They are having a party to celebrate the upcoming wedding, and we planned in the script to have a taffy pull, and the townspeople get so entangled in the taffy that our group can make their getaway and save Ernie from his sacrifice. We made taffy, but found when we tried it that the idea didn't work, so a square dance was substituted. Ernie called the square dance, and

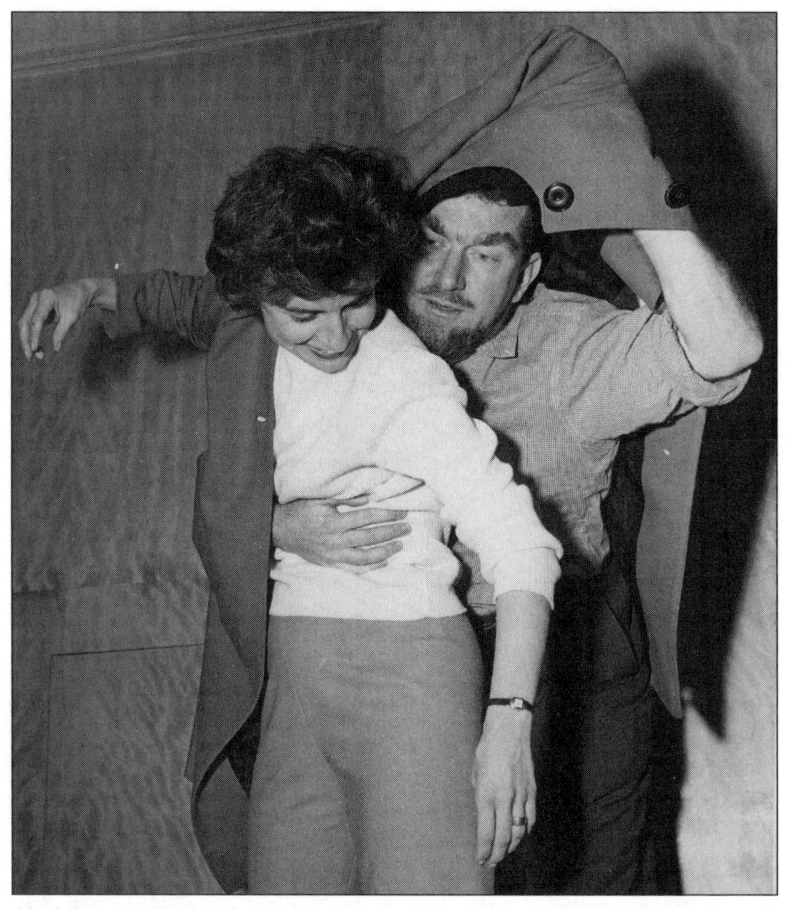

Madelyn and Bob work out the overcoat routine from "Lucy Wants A Career" episode of The Lucille Ball-Desi Arnaz Show.

when the Sheriff, Teensie, Weensie, and a cousin of Ernie's (played by a very funny young actor named Aaron Spelling, who wasn't a TV tycoon yet) are in the center of the dance, our foursome take ropes and by do-si-doing around them, tie them up and make their escape.

In many cases, THE BLACK STUFF was just a blueprint for Lucy. She would do what we had written and then add brilliantly to it.

An example of that is known as "Vitameatavegamin," actually titled "Lucy Does a TV Commercial," which was directed by Marc Daniels. Every move Lucy made was carefully written out in THE BLACK STUFF. Joe, the stage manager, played by Jerry Hausner, looks at the bottle of Vitameatavegamin and notes that it is 23% alcohol. Lucy arrives and the "director," played by Ross Elliott, runs through the commercial with her.

DIRECTOR

Now, let's go, and remember, be bright and vivacious.

From when Lucy begins to "rehearse" the commercial, doing it over many times, sampling the tonic and getting a little more tipsy each time, to where she is helped off the stage by the stage manager, the time is nine minutes and forty-nine seconds. Lucy did it straight through, in front of an audience, without cue cards, exactly as it was written. It should be noted, though, that all we wrote for the first time she tasted the tonic was:

LUCY TAKES THE TOP OFF THE BOTTLE AND POURS A TABLESPOON OF LIQUID.

LUCY

It's so tasty, too!

SHE SWALLOWS THE SPOONFUL WITH A BIG SMILE, THEN MAKES AN AWFUL FACE.

LUCY (CONT'D)

... Just like candy.

Of course, what Lucy did with "MAKES AN AWFUL FACE" was a classic of comedy reaction and had nothing to do with our writing.

Incidentally, the name "Vitameatavegamin" sounds like something you might find on the shelf in your local health

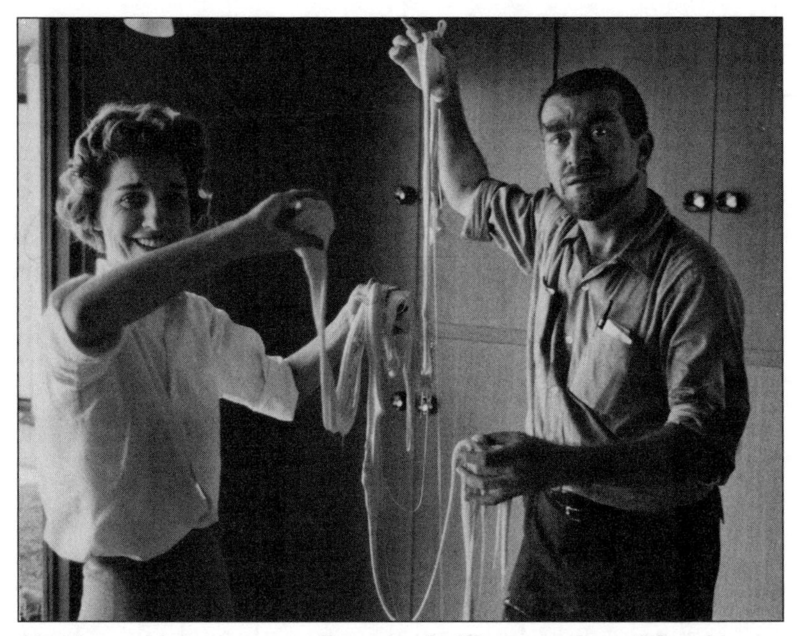

Madelyn and Bob try out a taffy routine for "Tennessee Bound" from I Love Lucy. *The taffy didn't work, and rope was used instead in the plot to facilitate an escape.*

food store, but the name took us a day and a half to come up with, and it was worth it. Another name that took us awhile was "All-Pet" for "The Business Manager" episode. We needed a name that sounded like pet food but also sounded like a company that could be on the stock market, so when Lucy wrote "Can All-Pet," Ricky mistakenly thought it was Canadian Allied Petroleum. I have read somewhere that the name for the product was added on the set. Well, not really. We never ever sent a script to the set with a notation saying, "Think up your own name."

In "Lucy Fakes Illness," we had to spend some time thinking up a rare fictional disease. Lucy wants to be in one of Ricky's shows and pretends to be having a nervous breakdown if he won't let her. He is very worried, but then finds out that she is faking it and, to teach her a lesson, gets an actor friend (Hal March) to pretend to be a doctor and tell her she is really sick. The doctor tells her she has a case of a little-known disease called the "go-bloots" (a name that took all afternoon). Dann Cahn told me whenever someone in the editing room wasn't feeling well, they used to say, "Maybe you have the go-bloots." And the worst thing was, it was hard to cure because "it was brought into this country on the hind legs of the boo-shoo bird." ("Boo-shoo" took half an hour.)

Another example of how Lucy added to the directions we gave her was in "Job Switching," which people call "The Candy Show." This is the one where Lucy and Ethel end up on an assembly line in a candy factory. Most of the action in THE BLACK STUFF is written out, but by the time the scene was filmed in front of the cameras, some things were added either by the director, Bill Asher, or Lucy and Viv. The inspired bits were Lucy and Ethel having their mouths crammed with candy when the Foreman (played so well by Elvia Allman) came in to inspect how they were doing, and Lucy hiding candy in her hat and putting the hat back on, with the telltale bulge hanging over her eyes. There were no chocolates left on the assembly line belt, which meant they were doing a good job, so the Foreman yelled to someone off stage.

FOREMAN

Speed it up a little!

One of the real advantages of writing for Lucille Ball was that she was absolutely fearless. Besides the many outrageous stunts we asked her to do, she was also "flown" many times like Peter Pan, that is, attached to wires and lifted high up in the air by professional "fliers." I can remember one show, "Ricky's Life Story," where she was on wires behind Ricky while he is doing a number at the club, and she turns upside down, while he is unaware of what is happening behind him. Later, during dinner served on the set between rehearsal and the show, I was sitting opposite her and she suddenly looked pale and fell over in a faint. Of course, she went on and did the show anyway. Jerry Hausner recalled an episode we did at the time Lucy was pregnant when she had to jump up and down on a bed. He says she went backstage, threw up, and came back to rehearsal.

We learned never to have the actress Lucille Ball look as if she were in danger in front of the audience. Lucy the character was outside of the apartment building on a ledge eight feet off the ground when she pretended to slip and almost fall while trying to go around a drain pipe in "Lucy and Superman." The studio audience gasped and didn't think it was funny, assuming it was an accident and not part of the script, and thought Lucy really was in danger.

And Lucy didn't mind working with animals. Thank goodness I didn't have to try those routines out because the animals weren't available, since they weren't on salary when we were writing the scripts. She worked with chimps, pigeons, penguins, baby chickens, burros, dogs, horses, dead tunas, and once sang a sheep to sleep while holding it on her lap. In the show titled "Lucy at Marineland," written by Bob O'Brien and directed by Maury Thompson, they actually went to Marineland, and Lucy happily got in the tank with several very large porpoises. One of the porpoises took a fancy to Lucy and became a little too friendly. She stood it as long as she could and when he got too close she yelled, "Get me out of here!" As they were getting her out of the pool, Maury says the porpoise gave Lucy a little nudge on her backside to help her out.

Tommy Thompson told me that when he was producing *The Lucy Show,* Lucy remarked to him that she had never worked with a lion and maybe that might make an interesting script. So he went to a lion farm out in the San Fernando Valley and interviewed lions. He said the trainer assured him that one in particular was very gentle and had worked with lots of stars. Tommy said he was standing there, minding his own business, when the "gentle" lion came up and fastened his arm in a firm, toothy grip, wouldn't let go, and had to be pried off. He went back to the studio and Lucy asked, "Did you find a lion?" Tommy told her, "Yes, only he tried to bite my arm off!" Lucy said, "But can he do comedy?"

I can only recall one time when Lucy balked at doing a stunt. It was in an episode called "Lucy Misplaces Two Thousand Dollars" in *The Lucy Show.* She is overdrawn at the bank by two dollars and has an argument with her banker, played by Charlie Lane. She claims it is the bank's mistake, and the banker points out it is her math that is at fault and tells her that banks don't make mistakes. Lucy becomes insulted and withdraws her Christmas account. The teller makes an error and gives Lucy $2,000 instead of twenty. Lucy decides to cash the check to teach the banker a lesson and plans to give back the four $500 bills later.

Through a series of mishaps, the money is lost at a carnival, and one of the bills ends up under an elephant's foot. We wrote a routine where Lucy works with the elephant to retrieve the bill. The first day of rehearsal, Bob and I arrived on the set, and the elephant was there, and somehow it was a lot bigger than we thought it was going to be. It was also weaving back and forth, like elephants do, checking out the territory with its trunk. All I could think of was what if he accidentally leaned on you? Lucy came on the set, walked up to the elephant, gave it one terrified look, and bolted to her dressing room. Word was sent to us that she didn't want to do the elephant scene. I couldn't blame her. I wouldn't want to either. So we trudged back

Lucy meets an elephant in "Lucy Misplaces Two Thousand Dollars" from The Lucy Show.

to the office to get another ending for the show since this was the big last scene. The three Bobs and I were thinking hard, with no new ideas at all, when Vivian called. She said,

"It's okay, Lucy's going to do it." I asked how come. Vivian said, "I told her if you don't want to do that funny bit with the elephant, I'll do it." And, of course, Lucy did the bit, lifting the elephant's foot and talking into his trunk. It was hilarious, and you would have thought she'd known that elephant all her life. It was the only time she ever flinched, and it was only a mini-flinch.

We often did research for the shows to be sure they were authentic, but mostly because it gave us good ideas. We went to New York and were shown around suburban Connecticut by CBS Vice President Hubbell Robinson. He pointed out an estate where the owner kept sheep on the huge front lawn to keep the grass down. This was the idea that became "Lucy Buys a Sheep" in *The Lucy Show.* For "Lucy and Her Electric Mattress" in the same series, Bob and I went to a department store and lay down on a mattress that vibrated, getting some strange looks from other customers. We went to an appliance store and looked at freezers to see if Lucy could get locked inside and come out almost frozen and dripping with icicles in "The Freezer."

In the episode where Lucy and Gale Gordon are locked in a bank vault all night, Bob and I visited a bank near the studio and we asked questions about how the automatic timer worked. They were quite helpful. Bob later confessed he had an irresistible impulse to say, "This is a stick-up," but restrained himself. We were awfully glad he did because we learned that everyone was quite edgy since there had been a real hold-up at the bank two days before, and we might have done some research on how it felt to be in a real jail.

Sometimes we would start working on a story line by saying, "What does Lucy want?" This could be she wants to go into show business, she wants new furniture, she wants to move to the country, to go into a small business venture, or meet a movie star. Sometimes we would have an idea for a large physical routine for Lucy and then figure a story that would get her there.

People often ask writers, "Where do you get your ideas?" My first impulse is to do what my kids used to do when I asked them, "Who was playing ball in the house and broke the lamp?" They would hunch up their shoulders and say, "I-un-know." I really can't explain it. One minute you're looking out the window, wondering if it's time for lunch, and the next minute you have an idea. Frankly, I-un-know. Of course, writing for a sitcom and having to do a show every week is a different kind of writing than doing a screenplay about a dinosaur or a serious novel about the Civil War. You write about people and their everyday lives and problems. You draw from your own experiences, things that happened to your friends or your fellow writers. Turning out a show each week doesn't leave you much time to stare out the window or even to have lunch. When you write a TV series, you use every scrap of material. Nothing goes to waste, sort of like making sausage.

We used everything we possibly could that happened to the writers. "Lucy Changes Her Mind" was based on what happened to Bob, Jess, and me while we were having lunch at The Brown Derby restaurant. I ordered a chicken sandwich. Then Bob ordered veal chops, and I changed my mind and said, "I'll have the chops." Then Jess ordered roast beef and I said, "Hey, that sounds good. I'll have the roast beef." We all looked at each other and a scene was born. Jess actually being bald and having tried all sorts of hair-restoring remedies led to the show "Ricky Thinks He is Going Bald." Desi loved going to the races, and I suspect bought a house on the ocean in Del Mar just so he could go across the road to the track. Johnny Longden, the jockey, was a good friend of his, which lead to his being a guest on "Lucy and the Loving Cup."

I went back to Indiana to visit an old friend of mine, Betty Rae Ricke, and she gave a dinner party for me. I was still single at that time, and I couldn't help noticing that the husbands were all talking together in the kitchen and the wives were all talking to each other in the living room. We made this a scene in "Charm School" carrying it a step further by having a single man (Maury Hill), bring a beautiful single girl (Eve Whitney) as his date, and all the husbands came out of the kitchen, much to their wives' disgust. Lucy and Ethel decided their problem was they needed to have more glamour and went to a charm school run by actress Natalie Schafer, later Lovey Howell of *Gilligan's Island.*

We heard that Lucy played the saxophone when she was a kid, so we asked her if she could play "Glow Worm" on the sax. "No," she said, "but give me two weeks." This became the episode "The Saxophone." We learned that Lucy could do almost anything if you gave her two weeks to work on it.

Since Bill Frawley had been in vaudeville, we wrote a script where his old partner Kurtz comes to town. We dubbed the act "Laugh till it hurts with Mertz and Kurtz." Kurtz was played by Charles Winninger.

Vivian once suggested maybe the Mertzes could have some newer furniture, so we wrote "Redecorating the Mertzes' Apartment." Lucy and Ethel paint the walls and then rip the cover off Fred's favorite chair. They find out it is full of feathers and guess what stuck to all the newly painted walls. For weeks after that, we would be reading a script and little feathers would waft down from high up in the catwalks of the stage.

"Men Are Messy" was undoubtedly based on our lives as a team. Bob and I worked at two desks, facing each other, and the desks were a good example of personalities. I have always maintained that Bob is neurotically messy, and he claims I am neurotically neat.

Some of our shows came from things that happened to our relatives. My cousin Martha had two sons, and she developed a habit of not getting up early enough to get dressed, make them breakfast and lunches, and drive them to school. Something had to give, so, of course, it was getting dressed. She used to drive them to school in her bathrobe. In *The Lucy Show,* Lucy, wearing her bathrobe for the same reason, is driving her kids to school and sees a butterfly that her son Jerry needs for a school project, jumps out of the car and eventually ends up in court in her bathrobe.

Bob Schiller confessed one day that he always thought people were going to give him a surprise party on his birthday and prepared himself to look as if he didn't expect it. This became the basis for an episode where Lucy mistakenly thinks Vivian and Betty Ramsey are going to give them a surprise housewarming. She and Ricky get all dressed up and practice having one of them jumping out of the closet yelling "surprise," while the other one practices looking totally dumbfounded.

The idea for "Nursery School" came from Bob Weiskopf's life. His son Kim was in the hospital, and his wife Eileen took him his favorite teddy bear, wrapped in a blanket, and the nurse thought it was a new baby that Eileen was bringing to the ER. In our version, Little Ricky was having his tonsils out, and Lucy was trying to sneak into the hospital to spend the night with him, which was against the rules at that time. She had his teddy bear hidden under her coat and the nurse thought she was pregnant and rushed her to the delivery room.

When I was divorced, well-meaning friends were fixing me up with blind dates. Some of these found their way into the scripts of *The Lucy Show* where Lucy and Vivian were both single. One of these was an attractive man I was seeing who was obsessed with sports and was always away on

Lucy collects a group of penguins on Here's Lucy.

weekends deer hunting or something. We drifted apart. It was just as well because I didn't want bits of Bambi in my freezer.

At one point I was giving a fifth birthday party for Michael. I picked up some balloons at the toy store, filled them with helium, and then tried to get them all in the car without having them float in front of my face while I was driving.

We used the balloons in "Kiddie Parties, Incorporated" in *The Lucy Show.* Lucy and Vivian have gone into the business of giving birthday parties for children. Lucy has to substitute for the clown she has hired who got sick, and when she starts to hand out helium balloons, they carry her up into the air, and she floats out of sight. Vivian has just called the Mayor and told him there have been various Lucy sightings around town and that he has to do something to bring her down when Lucy staggers in.

LUCY IS DISHEVELED. SHE'S LOST HER HAT AND ONE OF HER BIG CLOWN SHOES. HER COAT IS TORN, ETC. SHE IS CLUTCHING A BALLOON AND A WHOLE BUNCH OF STRINGS, SOME OF WHICH HAVE REMNANTS OF BALLOONS ON THEM. SHE LURCHES INTO THE ROOM.

VIVIAN

(DELIGHTED) Lucy!

LUCY

Boy. This space travel sure isn't what it's cracked up to be!

VIVIAN

Are you all right?

LUCY

I think so. I got sort of used to being up there. I even dozed off on my second orbit over Danfield.

VIVIAN

You poor little thing.

LUCY

You haven't lived until you've drifted sideways through a flock of geese!

So we used everything that ever happened to any of us for stories. Sometimes we would wander around the huge old prop department at Desilu-Gower, formerly RKO Studios, checking out if we could find a story line for a pogo stick or a stuffed gorilla. Of course, since Lucy would do absolutely anything we could think up, it gave us total creative freedom. Nothing was too difficult or too wild. Some sitcom writers may hope each week to do a heartfelt episode which is funny but really relevant and "about something." We often started our plotting sessions by saying, "Is there anything new we haven't done to Lucy?"

THIRTEEN

I'm Going Over to the Pope's House

I DON'T KNOW WHY IT IS, BUT I NEVER QUITE GOT over my awe of stars. No matter how many famous people I met, there was always a small voice inside saying, "Well, la-di-dah, get you!" I found myself struck dumb when Lucy introduced me to her next-door neighbor Jimmy Stewart outside her home in Beverly Hills one evening. He was walking his dog. How glamorous is that? And when John Wayne was a guest on *I Love Lucy* and I found myself sitting next to him at rehearsal, I'm embarrassed to admit it, but I babbled. They're just people like you and me, right? Well, not exactly. If I were like Lucille Ball, I would have buses going by my house with tourists hanging out the windows trying to get a glimpse of me. Lucy claimed fans used to come up and ring her doorbell, and she would answer the door, not wearing makeup and with her hair not done, and tell them she wasn't home. Well, she claimed that, anyway.

Through the years I was on a hugging relationship with Lucy—often when she was pleased with the script, I was locked in an embrace in which I couldn't get my breath. You'd think, wouldn't you, that I would relax and feel as if we were a couple of old shoes. Mary Wickes, the marvelous character actor, had that kind of relationship with her. Mary played the ballet teacher in *I Love Lucy* and made seventeen appearances on the various Lucy shows plus more than sixty roles on other TV programs, more than forty movies, and many Broadway productions. Mary and Lucy used to go careening around town in an old Rolls Royce that once belonged to Hedda Hopper. One time when they were out past dark, Lucy, who didn't drive often, couldn't remember how to turn on the lights, and they were stopped by the police. After the police drove off, she still couldn't find the lights, so she and Mary drove home in the dark, with Mary leaning out the window and yelling out potential hazards. For some reason, Mary used to call Lucy "Bertha Mae." Elliott Lewis called her "Big Red," and Jack Donohoe, her director, called her "Louise." I didn't exactly call her "Miss Ball," and I was very fond of her, but as long as I knew her, I never quite took the whole thing in stride. All I know is when I was invited to Lucy's for dinner, I had trouble telling people where I was going. It was like saying, "I'm going over to the Pope's house."

Maybe the reason I find celebrities so awe-inspiring is that I personally have the kind of looks that blend into a crowd. Bob Carroll, on the other hand, is immediately recognizable. When we were writing *I Love Lucy*, his hair and beard were red, and it was before beards were really popular, so people always remembered him. They only remembered me if I was standing next to him. I would have made a good spy or bank robber. "Did you get a good look at her?" "Well, she was medium height, not fat or thin, brownish hair, you know, average."

I once thought I had the basis for some kind of article about celebrities I had encountered. I was going to call it "Men I Have Met in Their Bathrobes." This may not seem like such a big deal today when high-powered producers have business meetings in T-shirts and jeans, but men used to conduct business wearing suits and ties, so a bathrobe was a little unusual. My list included Desi. When Bob and I were writing *The Mothers-in-Law* series, Desi kept an apartment at the studio. He and his wife Edie would stay at the studio during the week and go to their home in Del Mar, California, over the weekend. So he would often wander down the hall to our office in the morning wearing his p.j.s and bathrobe to discuss things with us while he had his coffee.

Then there was Harry Karl, Debbie Reynolds' husband at that time. We were being considered as writers for Debbie's TV show and went over to her house to be interviewed. During the interview, Mr. Karl joined us. He was wearing a robe and not much else, although I couldn't be sure since I kept my eyes glued to Debbie's face because I didn't want to find out.

When Bob and I went back to Washington, D.C., on our ill-fated attempt to "fix" the Broadway musical *Hot Spot,* we had another of our bathrobe encounters. This time it was Morton DaCosta. We had a meeting with him about the show while he was wearing his bathrobe and sitting in the middle of his hotel bed. This was actually legitimate, though, because he was not well at the time.

Another citing of a star in his bathrobe was when Bob and I did a tour of the movie stars' homes to get material for "The Tour" script when the Ricardos went to Hollywood. This time it was Pat O'Brien. Movie buffs will remember him for his many films, including *Knute Rockne, All-American,* in which he told the young actor Ronald Reagan "to win one for the gipper." Pat O'Brien was the highlight of the tour

Mary Wickes tries to make a ballerina out of Lucy.

as he appeared in his bathrobe on his way to the mailbox to collect his mail. I'm not sure this counts, either, as it was only a cameo appearance. Anyway, I gave up the idea of doing an article because, as they say in publishing circles, "it has limited appeal," and besides, today it would only sell if it were "Men I Have Met in the Nude" and that was pretty much out of the question.

One of the most unforgettable afternoons I ever spent was with Gypsy Rose Lee. She was the actress and former stripper, probably best known for her autobiography *Gypsy*, which was later turned into the hugely successful Broadway musical starring Ethel Merman, a movie with Rosalind Russell, a TV special with Bette Midler, and a stage revival with Bernadette Peters. Desi had an idea for a series with Gypsy, so the three of us went to her house in Beverly Hills one afternoon. I hadn't met a lot of strippers, so it was another one of those "la-di-dah" moments. Gypsy was very charming and didn't remove a single article of clothing while we were there. She wasn't wearing stockings, however, and I soon found out why. She adored dogs, and her current favorite in residence was a Chinese Hairless, who had just had three puppies. The puppies were so small they had trouble getting up the two steps that led to the living room. They were, however, big enough so when they tried to get up on my lap, their little toenails were even with my pantyhose. It wasn't long before my stockings were hanging in shreds. Gypsy never mentioned it, and I pretended that multiple runs were a fashion statement. After we discussed the pilot, we had tea and cookies in the dining room. One whole wall that was a gigantic birdcage with all sorts of colorful species flitting about. Desi and Bob and I dutifully admired the birds, which pleased her, because as she explained, "Some people don't like to eat in the middle of all that birdshit."

I think the trouble with meeting big stars is that they look just like you think they're going to. You might assume when they don't have makeup people or hairdressers fussing over them, they won't look so hot. Maybe they even have a bad hair day or a zit. But they look just like they look up there on the screen—only smaller. When you are reading a script while you are sitting next to Bob Hope, Rock Hudson, or Orson Welles, it's hard to be nonchalant.

When we were assembling to have a script reading of

Rock Hudson helps the Ricardos and the Mertzes reconcile.

"Lucy Meets the Burtons" in Desi's office, I was standing with my back to the door, talking to Lucy's assistant Wanda, when a sort of hush descended over the room. I turned around and was face to face with the gorgeous Miss Taylor, who was making her entrance. And I swear her eyes really were lavender.

I was dumbstruck when I met Bette Davis. We wanted her and her husband Gary Merrill to do a Lucy-Desi Hour called "The Celebrities Next Door," and she said she would like to hear the story line before agreeing to do it. Bob Carroll, Bob Schiller, Bob Weiskopf, and I went trooping out to her agent's office to pitch our idea. I had seen every one of her movies and can clearly remember coming out of the theater feeling as if I were doing that famous switchy walk of hers. So I was pretty excited.

Now, I was working with three bright and articulate men, and Bob Weiskopf had even been the Merrill's neighbor in Connecticut, but for some reason I was the designated pitcher. I always seem to land this role. "You're so good at it," they'd say, which is another way of saying, "And I don't want to do it." "Pitching" is something writers have to do if they want to sell a pilot to a grim-faced network executive or an idea for a movie to a bored studio development head. Personally, I would rather have a mammogram. I have heard that in the old studio days, there would be a writing team and then a third man who was good at telling stories, and he was the one who pitched the story to Irving Thalberg or Darryl Zanuck or whoever. The third man was known as the Scheherazade.

Anyway, we go into the office and there she was, looking like Bette Davis, talking like Bette Davis, and smoking like Bette Davis. She had her hair in pigtails and was wearing a summer dress and looked very young and pretty, and after a few opening remarks, she said, "So what's this show about?" and fastened me with those big Bette Davis eyes. I did my Scheherazade number, and it must have been okay because later her agent called and said she and Gary would like to do the show. Unfortunately, things at their house weren't working out so smoothly, and the Merrills picked that time to get a divorce, so we had to forget about them as the couple next door.

Kathleen Hite, the writer I shared an office with at CBS when I first came to Hollywood, confessed that she, too, suffered from the "la-di-dah" complex, and she also had a Bette Davis story. She had worked with the star in a TV anthology series Kathleen had written. Bette and Gary were later doing a reading of *The Wonderful World of Carl Sandburg* at the old Huntington Hartford Theater in Hollywood, so Kathleen decided to see the show with her friend Marian Clark, who incidentally was the first woman news writer hired by CBS on the West Coast. At the time, Marian was in a wheelchair, so when Kathleen went backstage after the show, Marian couldn't go up the stairs to the dressing rooms and waited below. She urged Kathleen to go without her, saying that she had met a lot of big people in show business and stars didn't really mean a thing to her. Kathleen saw Bette and said all the complimentary things about the performance, and then Bette said, "You didn't come alone?" Kathleen explained about her friend in the wheelchair, and Bette flew down the stairs to meet her. Kathleen said that Marian, to whom stars didn't mean a thing, said, "Oh, Miss Davis, it's a real thrill for you to meet me."

Kathleen also had an unnerving experience with Gloria Swanson. Miss Swanson had been a big star in early movies and had just made a huge comeback receiving an Academy Award nomination for *Sunset Boulevard.* An anthology series called *Crown Theater* was being planned, a half hour of drama, with a well-known star doing openings and closings. This was a popular form on TV at the time, with Loretta Young, Jane Wyman, Alfred Hitchcock, and even future President Ronald Reagan as the host and occasional guest star. The producers hired Miss Swanson and wanted Kathleen to write some of the scripts and the clever "ad-libs" for the host, what used to be called "gazintas" as in "goes intos." The only problem was, Miss Swanson hadn't worked with a woman writer before and wasn't sure she liked the idea. So the producers ran some of Kathleen's shows for her and introduced them to each other, and apparently Kathleen passed the test.

Miss Swanson told her she wanted to work closely with her at her house. "I'm staying at Rudy's old place," she said. Kathleen later asked one of the producers just what "Rudy's old place" might be, and he explained it was Rudolph Valentino's old home called "Falcon's Lair," up in the hills. Kathleen said she spent so much time in Miss Swanson's house, she felt as if she was the butler, played by Erich von

Stroheim, in *Sunset Boulevard.*

She said her most unforgettable visit was the day she arrived at Rudy's Old Place, gazintas in hand, and the secretary told her Miss Swanson was in the lower garden doing her yoga exercises. So Kathleen made her way to the lower garden through the master bedroom, where she swears there was a chinchilla spread on the bed. What the secretary had neglected to mention was that Miss Swanson was doing her yoga exercises in the nude, wearing only a turban and a serene expression. Kathleen says she studied the terrain of Benedict Canyon below with such concentration, you would think she was trying to spot brush fires.

You have to be careful when you eat with stars. Kathleen told me that one of her sessions with Miss Swanson ran late one day, and she was invited to stay for dinner. The actress was a devout vegetarian before it became popular and Kathleen claims that the entire meal consisted of a bowl of blanched celery.

Desi once cooked or roasted or whatever you do to a suckling pig for a large group. I have a little trouble with food that still has its head on. I was afraid the pig was going to open one eye and say, "Th-th-that's all, folks!" Hoagy Carmichael and Bill Holden both offered me drinks at ten in the morning instead of coffee. Carol Channing wanted to share her dinner with Bob and me, and I can't be certain because we declined, but I think it was stewed grass. Apparently, Carol was allergic to a lot of foods and used to take her own dinner in a Thermos to banquets. Bob and I were planning to write a TV pilot for her for Desi's company, so we flew back to Chicago to see her in *Hello, Dolly!* and meet afterwards at her hotel. She was having a little green snack and whatever it was, it wasn't fattening because she was quite slender. She was wearing a dark blue sailor suit and since she was tall, she

Orson Welles does magic tricks and Lucy is his assistant.

looked sort of like a navy blue yardstick.

You have to be careful when you eat with directors, too. Bob and I were having lunch with Cleo Smith, the producer, and Coby Ruskin, the director of *Here's Lucy.* Cleo and Bob and I were eating off each other's plates, saying, "Can I have your pickle?," "Are you going to finish that?," "Can I have some of your French fries?," etc. Coby watched in distaste. "I'm never having lunch with you again." And he never did.

I don't want to give the impression that all the stars I have worked with are eccentric. Some of them are really like the people next door—like Eve Arden, if your next-door neighbor happens to be a lovely, talented woman who never gets mad and looks like a fashion model no matter what she happens to be wearing. In one episode of *The Mothers-In-Law,* Eve and Kaye Ballard were snooping in their kids' apartment when the kids come home unexpectedly, so they hide in the shower. Since this was a comedy show, Jerry decides to take a shower, reaches behind the curtain and turns on the water, and of course they were both soaked. After the dress rehearsal, we had a note session, and Eve appeared with a towel wrapped around her head like a turban, looking quite chic. Kaye, who wasn't looking exactly put together, couldn't stand it. "Look at her!" she fumed, "I hate her!"

Ethel Merman was a guest star in "Lucy Teaches Ethel Merman to Sing" in *The Lucy Show,* and even though Miss Merman was at that time a superstar on Broadway, she was also unpretentious. Her idea of being temperamental was to ask if she could change one word in the script and hold up a dress on a hanger, saying, "This is what I'm going to wear, and I'll do my own hair." Some years earlier on Broadway, Vivian Vance was the understudy for Merman in *Anything Goes,* a musical written by Cole Porter. Apparently, Ethel Merman was the kind of star who would crawl on her hands and knees to the theater rather than miss a performance, so Vivian only got to go on in her place twice. I was told about one of Merman's opening nights on Broadway. Just before the curtain went up, one of the kids in the chorus asked her, "Miss Merman, aren't you nervous?" and she answered in surprise, "Why should I be nervous? I know all the words."

FOURTEEN

Your Show's Only Half an Hour:

What Do You Do the Rest of the Week?

JESS OPPENHEIMER ONCE TOLD THE STORY OF BEING at a party and a woman came up to him and said, "I hear you're a writer. What have you written?" This was at the time when *I Love Lucy* was a huge hit, so Jess told her casually he was a producer-writer on *I Love Lucy* and stood back, waiting for the usual squeals of joy and the shower of compliments. "But your show's only half an hour," she said. "What do you do the rest of the week?"

When my friend the writer Larry Roman moved into a new house, he said the man next door greeted him with, "So you're a writer, what do you do in the daytime?"

People are very vague about just what it is a writer does. When it comes to television, they are only dimly aware that there ARE writers. You mean all that stuff is actually written down? And it is a no-win situation. The more natural your dialogue is, the more people think the actors are just talking to each other as they go along. Lately, the prices paid by movie studios for scripts have caught the public's attention. "Good Lord, Martha, some guy got paid a million dollars for just writing something!"

But even if they know there really are writers of movies and TV, people regard it as a rather strange occupation. I once sat next to a doctor at a dinner party, and we had a stimulating conversation about art and architecture and all sorts of things, and he asked me what I did. I said I was a television writer. He said, "My wife looks at that sometimes." When we left the table, he told me he had certainly enjoyed our conversation, and he looked forward to the day when I would maybe write a book.

Even writers' families aren't too clear about it. My mother had always encouraged me to be a writer, but I think she secretly thought it was a nice little hobby and was amazed people paid me for it. When I was on CBS's staff, I wrote radio shows all day, and then for several months I spent evenings at home ghost-writing a comedy spot for a friend of mine who was writing two shows at once. My mother was thrilled that I had an extra job and was getting paid for it. Or, as she put it "It's just like finding the money."

Moss Hart, the Broadway playwright, went to work at age seventeen as an office boy for a producer. He read so many bad plays that had been submitted, he decided he could do better. He sat down at the kitchen table and wrote what he said was a really terrible play. Surprisingly, the producer liked it and gave him a little bit of money as an advance. The next night, his mother cleared off the kitchen table and told him, "Now write another one." Later on, when he spent all his time off from his day job writing plays that he hoped to get produced, his mother referred to it as his "homework."

Lucy, Bob Carroll Jr., Bob Schiller, Madelyn, Bob Weiskopf and Desi discuss this week's I Love Lucy *script.*

Kathleen Hite told me a story about being at a family reunion at a remote lake in Minnesota. She had to write a script while she was there, but there wasn't any phone, so she would go into town to a general store to call the producer. There were also incoming wires and calls for her, and the storekeeper was very impressed and asked Kathleen's sister if Kathleen was really writing a script for Hollywood. Kathleen's sister explained, "Not really. All she's doing is adding the dialogue." And this was radio.

People also don't understand it if a writer is staring into space, as in thinking. Arthur Marx, author of twelve books including *Son of Groucho* and many plays and TV scripts with his partner Robert Fisher, told me this happened to him. When he first started his career, he was writing scripts for some short subjects at MGM. He said he was looking out the window when the producer walked by his office and said accusingly, "I didn't pay you to look out the window."

Amazingly, many actors are murky about what writers do. I was watching *The Golden Globe Awards* on TV recently, and the first four actors who received awards thanked "the cast and crew" who helped them win this coveted trophy. After the fourth time, I found myself yelling at the screen, "The writers! What about the writers?!" Now, Lucille Ball was one of those special performers who always gave her writers credit for her success at every opportunity. Nobody really believed her, but she kept saying it anyway. But let's be honest, many actors, after they have memorized the lines and thrown away the script, begin to think they made it up themselves and get amnesia about that white paper with the little printing on it that started the whole thing. I'm not talking about comics like Jerry Seinfeld, Sid Caesar, Paul Reiser, or Bill Cosby, who contributed a lot to the writing process. But sometimes actors on a series, who play the same role for years, begin to think their characters are making it all up. They give interviews where they imply that the ensemble cast actually ad-libs most of the show. I've been told that one group of comedy writers got so sick of hearing how the cast made everything up that when they sat down to do the first reading, there was a title page and forty-five blank pages. Then the writers said politely, "Okay, now make it up."

I can't explain it, but writers for movies and TV are pretty far down the creative food chain. If you write for the theater, you're an "author" and on opening night you may get a "bravo!" or a "brava!" or even a curtain call. But I heard one story about a female star who was showing some friends around the studio. When she came to one office, she announced, "This is where we keep our writers."

After the *Lucy* shows, we were producers of a sitcom, and our schedule was to tape three or four shows and then take a week off. The actors were quite pleased with this schedule and after a hiatus, one asked me, "Where did you go on your week off?" I gently explained that Bob and I went to our office and worked on scripts with the rest of the writers.

Let's face it, writers are very protective of their material. This is their child. Hence the expression "brain child" and nobody likes to hear "you have a very ugly baby." Earl Hamner, creator of *The Waltons* and *Little House on the Prairie,* was a big fan of Kathleen's writing, but he told me he once phoned her to discuss one of her *Waltons* scripts. Earl was the executive producer and for some valid reason he had rewritten her ending. He explained this to her, and he said there was a long pause. Then she said flatly, "Don't ever do that again."

We used to dread Monday mornings, which was when the cast saw the script for the first time as they read it aloud around the table. Bob used to refer to it as the "Monday mauling." It's not that they were super critical, but in fifty years of writing, I have never heard anybody say, "This is perfect. Don't change a thing." Reactions can range anywhere from loud laughter and appreciation to what happened on another show (thankfully not one we were connected with) where after the first reading, the star threw the script across the room, sneering, "Now show me the real script!" All I know is that we never became inured to those first readings and faced them with all the enthusiasm of heading for a car wreck.

Okay, so now if you are a writer who is blessed with a cast who thinks you write inspired dialogue and mentions you in interviews, you still have to deal with the opinions of producers and network executives. When the writer Frank Mula heard I was doing a chapter on the stupid things producers say to writers, he remarked, "Only one chapter?"

At one point, Desi asked us to meet with a Desilu producer and maybe we could all come up with an idea for a series starring Vivian Vance. We were kicking around some ideas

Bob Schiller, Bob Carroll Jr., Lucy, Desi, Madelyn, and Bob Weiskopf.

and the man said, "I've got it! Why don't we make Vivian a man!" Neither one of us had an answer for that.

On another occasion, we were writing for a Dinah Shore special and the producer suggested an idea for a sketch. Personally, we thought the idea was pretty bad, but since he seemed so pleased with it, we gave it a try. After we turned it in, he called us and said in his opinion the sketch didn't work. This was too much, even for us, and I blurted out, "But it was YOUR idea!" The producer explained it this way: "Oh, well, you guys can write anything."

Comedy writer Laura Levine said she had written a movie that a producer was interested in. Her script was about a demon who comes up from hell to corrupt the soul of an innocent woman, but winds up falling in love with her. In the movie, the woman has a dog. The producer hired a director who she says came up with this fabulous idea. Why not, in a zany twist, he suggested, have the dog turn out to be God since God is dog spelled backwards? Laura said, "Thank God, or should I say thank Dog, they didn't go for the idea."

Kathleen told me she did a script for a western drama about a young girl who was a mute and could communicate with animals. She lived on a ranch, and her favorite friend was a baby deer. When the deer was grown, a neighboring rancher was about to shoot it for food, and the girl ran to save the deer and was wounded. The producer loved the script, but was having trouble with the conflict. He thought perhaps a deer was a little dull. He asked, "Could you make the deer a grizzly?" Kathleen couldn't quite figure how a young girl could be best friends with a 300-pound grizzly bear.

Jimmie Komack was the producer of *My Favorite Martian* starring Ray Walston. He sent the network a copy of the current script, and it came back with this comment: "Please change the dialogue on page 14. A Martian wouldn't say that." This became the title of a book of quotes from executives' memos to writers compiled by Leonard B. Stern and Diane L. Robison, who swear they are authenticated. They have kindly given me permission to share some of them. (It was hard to choose.)

"I think you're making a mistake in having so many French involved in the production of *Les Miserables*."

"Can we make the Rabbi less Jewish?"

"When the nurses take a shower, do not have them nude."

"We must de-emphasize violence this season. Make the room red so the blood won't show."

And my all-time favorite from the vice president of programming to the producers of *The Fred Astaire Special*: "Too much dancing."

Of course, writers sometimes can be their own worst enemies. Long, long ago when there was no Xerox or computers, the only way you could make a copy of your script was to take it to a duplicating service where they used a device known as a mimeograph machine. Someone would type the whole script over on special duplicating paper and run it through the machine page by page to make copies. The networks used to have their own mimeo departments with rows of typists busily working. If you were just a writer and not a network, this was expensive and time consuming, so sometimes writers would have only one copy of the script. You can see where this is going. Kathleen Hite once threw out an entire hour script with the Christmas wrappings, went through all the trash and never did find it, and wrote the whole thing over. Robert Fisher lost the only copy of a book he was writing in the Bel-Air fire.

Bob and I were working on a movie script at my house late one night, and he left to take the finished version to an all-night mimeo service on his way home. I don't remember why it was our only copy because we were usually careful about this. It was a rewrite of a movie, and I think we had pasted the rewrite together with part of the original. He put it on top of his car along with some other things he was carrying, then unlocked his car and drove off. He heard a strange "plop" and for some unknown reason stopped to investigate, and found the script in the gutter. The movie was never made, so maybe this was an omen.

Garry Marshall, a movie writer and director, and creator-producer of many hit TV series, tells a similar story in his autobiography, *Wake Me When It's Funny*, written with his daughter Lori. He had completed his first movie script with his partner Jerry Belson. They were freelancing scripts for TV during the week, and on the weekends they spent all their time working on a screenplay, hoping to break into film. It was titled *Ciao,* and the story centered around a famous Italian actor, so they thought it would be perfect for Marcello Mastroianni. Jerry was going to Europe on a vacation, so

Bob Carroll Jr. (left) takes a break from writing to be an extra on the ship to Europe.

they decided he should make a stop in Italy and show the script to the famous star. The only trouble was somewhere in Europe, Jerry lost the script. In a taxi or a crowded airport, he never knew where. But the script was gone forever, and it was their only copy.

Larry Roman, who still does his work on a typewriter, told me he usually goes to lunch at a little coffee shop near his office. For protection, he always takes the only copy of his work in progress with him to lunch (I guess in case some script burglars ransacked his office). He says three times he has left the script on the counter at the coffee shop, and three times they have called him to tell him they have saved it for him. I heard that on Sid Caesar's *Show of Shows,* the script was left on a table in the writing room, and the cleaning lady threw it out. Michael Stewart, who thought it was his fault, went in early and wrote the script over, at least as much as he could remember.

I especially like the story told by Millie Tibbles, wife of George Tibbles, a playwright, who also did most of the scripts for the TV show *My Three Sons* starring Fred MacMurray. Millie says that George was flying to Phoenix from Palm Springs to help in rehearsals of one of his plays. He packed a briefcase with a tape recorder, an unfinished manuscript of another play, and some personal things for overnight. George, who could be a little absent-minded, left the briefcase sitting in the middle of the Palm Springs Airport. Right about this time, one of a terrorist's favorite things was to carry a bomb in a briefcase and leave it unattended somewhere. Airport security noticed the case, which had no nametag, only a sticker from a foreign country where George and Millie had visited. When they X-rayed it, it looked like some sort of mechanical device with cylinders and coils that could be a bomb (George's tape recorder) and a possible bottle of nitroglycerin (George's Old Spice). They called in the Marine Corps demolition squad from nearby Twentynine Palms, who took the briefcase out on the tarmac and blew it up along with George's only copy of his new play, which was now scattered all over Riverside County. The police delivered what was left of the briefcase to George's home, and by now Millie had talked to him and knew he was safe. She assured the officers that George was really quite harmless. She explained, "He's just a writer."

FIFTEEN

Don't Step on the Children

I WAS MARRIED FOR THE SECOND TIME IN 1964. When I tell people how I happened to get together with my husband, Dr. Richard Davis, they think it is terribly romantic and sometimes say things like "Awww!"

No matter what they claim, divorced women with young children are always looking for that second great guy who likes kids and would make a wonderful husband-slash-stepfather. When you have a small son, you hope to find someone who will do guy things with him like teach him how to throw a ball and go on those father-son Cub Scout weekends. Or, as in my son Michael's case, take him to the auto races and the Demolition Derby. No matter how good a mother you are, it's hard to get too excited about seeing Evel Knievel hurtle his motorcycle over eight parked cars. Michael's father, Quinn Martin, saw him twice a week and often took him to pony rides at the little track that used to be on the corner of

Madelyn and Dr. Richard Davis are married in Marion, Indiana.

La Cienega and Beverly Boulevard, now the Beverly Center. Quinn would watch the kids go round and round as he stood at the rail with all the other divorced dads. But he now had a new family and single moms will understand there are certain gaps that are hard to fill. Like what kind of vacation appeals to a 39-year-old woman and a 3-year-old boy? You can only go to the San Diego Zoo so many times. Somehow a mother and one child just don't add up to a whole family. There is obviously a reason why parents come in twos.

Bob would come and work at my house whenever he could. Of course, Michael wanted to be in on the action, so to keep him busy, Bob would draw large letters of the alphabet and Michael would go away and make them into animals. He turned out to be a talented artist, and maybe this encouraged him. Later, when I took him to the children's art class at the L.A. County Museum, he taught me something about how you treat artists. I picked him up after class, and he was carrying a large slab of cardboard on which were small lumps of something with straws stuck out at various angles. The entire thing was splashed with bright red paint. The lumps seemed to be leaning toward each other. I know you're not supposed to ask artists what their painting represents, but this time I couldn't resist. I assumed that the red was blood, the straws were weapons, and the title, when it was hung in a gallery, would be "War!" "Uh—what's it supposed to be?" I asked. "It's clay and straw and paint," he said, and added, "it fell off the table and that made it a lot better."

When he was old enough, I took him to see the shows I was working on, but I'm not certain he was too impressed. Kids aren't sure what all the fuss is about. I remember one rehearsal where Lucie and Desi Jr., were very young and visiting the set, and their mother told them, "If you go home and take a nap, you can stay up until nine and see the show," and Little Lucie said, "What show?"

Richard Crenna told me a story about being in China filming the movie *The Sand Pebbles* with Steve McQueen and Candice Bergen. Dick and his family were in a restaurant having dinner, and people kept glancing over. His little son asked, "Daddy, why are they looking at us?" And he answered, "Well, I guess they know who we are." His son said, "Who are we?"

Once, when Dick and I were babysitting our grandchildren, an *I Love Lucy* episode came on TV and the seven year old turned to me and announced importantly, "My mother knows the lady who wrote that show."

Back in the days when I was a single mom, I occasionally thought about getting married again. If I went out with a man for dinner a few times, I might think, "Is this IT?" It was rarely IT. Usually, it was a hundred miles from IT. I had just about put the idea aside and quit humming "The Second

Time Around," figuring I was never going to meet Mr. Right, when along came Dr. Definite Possibility.

The story begins once upon a time, long, long ago (I'll try to make this brief). Dick Davis and I were students at Indiana University. We had a "G-rated" little romance and "went steady" our junior year. "Went steady"—that'll give you an idea how long ago it was. We never even discussed getting married. I had plans for a career in journalism, and he was pre-med and going to be a doctor, which meant many years of training. Our senior year, we drifted apart, and he began going with Elaine Ax, also a student at IU whom he later married. He went to Philadelphia General Hospital for his internship and the Mayo Clinic for his residency. He was a captain in the Army Medical Corps during World War II, went back to Marion, Indiana, started the Davis Clinic with his father and brother Joseph, who were also doctors, and had four children. Meanwhile, I was doing my number in California.

Dick's wife, Elaine, died in 1962, and I sent him a sympathy note. I remember hesitating before I mailed it. I didn't want to look like one of those women who is waiting on the doorstep with a casserole when the widower comes home from the memorial service. But eventually I mailed the letter because I really felt bad about what he was going through. This was before e-mail, and you actually wrote something on a piece of paper, put it in an envelope with a stamp on it, and dropped it in the mailbox. And then you often got an envelope of your own back. Well, this sort of thing went on for sometime, with letters back and forth and lots of phone calls. On one of these, Dick said something which has stayed with me ever since. He was a surgeon and on call at the local hospital emergency room every other night. It was about 10 p.m. California time and 1 A.M. his time when the operator broke in and said he had an emergency call. He had to go to the hospital and said he'd phone me back, which he did about

Madelyn and Dr. Richard Davis at their west coast wedding reception at the Bel Air Hotel, with their son Michael.

an hour later. Being a dedicated insomniac, I was in awe. I asked him how can you just go take care of an emergency call and then come home and go right back to sleep? He thought it over. "Well," he explained, "if you're standing up you're awake, and if you're lying down, you're asleep."

After a while, we decided if we were going to talk on the phone for two hours every night, maybe we should meet in Chicago, so we did. Now, every woman knows that meeting an old boyfriend after twenty years and thinking you're going to rekindle any sort of spark is pretty pathetic. You are certain you're going to look at him and say, "Who is this person? Yuk!" Amazingly enough, the kindling went very well, and we didn't say "Yuk!" at all. It was more of a middle-aged "wow."

Old school friends in Indiana kept telling Dick that I was divorced, and he should look me up, and Dick played it cool and didn't say we were corresponding and said, "Well, maybe." Later that year, we got together again in San Francisco, where Dick could use the meeting of the American College of Surgeons as a cover. Bob Carroll flew up, too, and while Dick went to meetings, we worked on the script for "Lucy Teaches Ethel Merman to Sing."

We managed to put Dick's name in a script where Lucy has an encounter with a Dr. Davis in "Lucy is Florence Nightingale." One weekend Michael and I went back and met Dick, his kids and his parents in Chicago. Dick's children were Brian, age 15, Charlotte, 12, Lisa, 8, and Ned, 6. It had been snowing and some of the cars were still covered. My five-year-old son, a real product of California and show business, wanted to know if the snow was real, thinking maybe it was fake and done by special effects.

That December, right after Christmas, Dick brought his children to Los Angeles for a visit. I tried to strike a blow for wicked stepmothers everywhere by arranging a limo trip to the Rose Parade and taking everyone to Disneyland. Apparently, I did a good selling job because Dick's children were most enthusiastic about the whole idea of our getting married. Brian's comment was, "What are we waiting for? Let's get this show on the road!" And my son, Michael, said, "Oh, boy, you mean I'm going to have a family?" We became engaged and planned a wedding for May, and then Michael and I would move back to Indiana.

I told Lucy my news, and she was very pleased for me, and it worked out for her schedule as well. We were winding up the 1963-64 season of *The Lucy Show*, and she had decided that she wouldn't continue with a series. This was pretty much a spring ritual with her. She would be tired at the end of the season and wanted to get out of the grind of doing a weekly show. Ross Dowd, then our set designer, said at these times Lucy eventually would get bored and want to redecorate her whole house, and he dreaded when she was on hiatus.

Even though Lucy claimed she wouldn't ever do another series, she was at that time president of Desilu, so she got talked into using her own shows as leverage to sell other Desilu pilots, and after she was rested, she would agree to another season. She was also happiest when she was performing. But at this time, it worked out neatly. We were both embarking on second marriages, Schiller and Weiskopf were going to write *The Red Skelton Show*, Bob was going to live in Europe for a while, and I was going to live in Indiana. It was time to move on.

My California friends were thrilled I was getting married, but they were a little vague about where I was going to live. One of those states that begins with a vowel like Iowa or Ohio, right? I would carefully explain, "Now, you've heard of the Indy 500..."

Dick had told his parents and his brother that he was getting married, and he was planning to make an announcement to the other partners in the Davis Clinic who, if they heard the news at random, might feel it was somehow the end of the Davis Clinic and Dick was moving away. You know how gossip goes. But the syndicated columnist Hedda Hopper spilled the beans. I had run into her one day when I was leaving Lucy's house and she was arriving. Lucy told her my news, and it never dawned on me that Hedda would think this was worth mentioning in her column, with a headline:

JUST LIKE THE MOVIES

> "Madelyn Pugh Martin, Lucille Ball's writer for lo these many years, is retiring from the show to start a beautiful new life. At the end of May, she'll be married to Dr. Richard Davis and move into a Frank Lloyd Wright house in Marion, Indiana, where the doctor and his brother head the Davis Clinic. They were sweethearts in college, but he went on to medical school and she with her career. Both married other people. Madelyn got a divorce. She has a boy, 6, and the doctor's wife died, leaving four children in age from 15 to 6½. After twenty years, the two met again, and are now busy writing the happy ending to their story. Madelyn will continue writing, plans a play, and some movie scripts. Her own yarn would make a dandy picture."

Hedda's syndicated column wasn't carried in the local Marion paper, but it was carried in the *Chicago Tribune*, and when Dick went to the Clinic that morning, one of the partners was having coffee and reading the *Tribune*, looked up and said, "Congratulations."

Dick and I were married May 23, 1964. The night before Michael and I were to fly back to Marion for the wedding, Bob and I were finishing a script at my house. Our agent Marvin Moss thought it would be a good idea if we had one more movie credit so that Bob and I could write an occasional script for the movies from my new location. We were rewriting something for Universal called *The Welcome Wagon Lady*, almost finished, and doing the last scene. There was a sticky plot point about how somebody got out from behind the Iron Curtain. I have totally blacked out on why a Welcome Wagon Lady was behind the Iron Curtain, but all I know is we planned to use whatever ruse the former writers had written. We came to this dreaded portion and guess what. One character said to the other, "How did you get out from behind the Iron Curtain?" And the other character said, "Don't ask." It is now one o'clock in the morning and I still have to pack and wash my hair and get an early plane. We held our respective noses, put down "Don't ask," and finished the script. The movie was never made (what a surprise), but who cared, I was getting married.

It was a small wedding with Brian as Dick's best man and only our family and a few very close friends attending, followed by a luncheon. Lucy called the Marion florist and ordered yellow tulips, one of her favorite flowers, for the centerpiece. The florist almost had a nervous breakdown. Lucille Ball had ordered tulips, and there were no tulips to be had for miles around. So they substituted yellow roses, and I thanked Lucy for the yellow tulips. We came back to Los Angeles, had a wedding reception at the Bel Air Hotel, dropped Michael at his father's, and went on a one-week honeymoon driving to San Francisco, planned by my resident travel expert, Bob Carroll.

On our way up the coast, we stayed overnight in Carmel and I called the Beardsleys (the family of *Yours, Mine and Ours* fame) and we went over to their house. Helen and Frank weren't there, but a nun, Frank's sister, was keeping an eye on things. One of the kids explained that their mother and father were away for the weekend. She said they had taken five of the kids with them. She explained those five were "the trouble-makers."

We returned to Los Angeles after our honeymoon. We picked up Michael at his father's home and went back to Marion, Indiana, to settle down in Dick's house. I suddenly had five children instead of one. I went around for weeks with that glazed expression you see on the faces of mothers in the hospital who had just given birth to quadruplets like, "I'm really thrilled, but what just happened here?"

I was blessed with two wonderful mothers-in-law. Later, Bob and I wrote a series called *The Mothers-in-Law,* but it had nothing to do with my real life. The mothers-in-law in the show were the kind who butted into their children's lives because butting in is funnier than butting out. Quinn's mother, Ann Cohn, whom I called Annie, was a good friend, and after Quinn and I were divorced, she used to babysit while I went out on dates. Quinn's late father Martin was a film editor and producer, so she was interested in the business and each year I gave her a subscription to *Daily Variety*. She was still reading *Variety* when she was in her 90s and talking to me about TV ratings and film grosses.

Dick's mother's real name was Josephine, but everybody called her "Boo." She was a former concert pianist and the kind of woman who formed the first chapter of The League of Women Voters in Marion. In 1937, she started the Marion Easter Pageant, which is still in existence today. This is a series of Biblical tableaus and Easter music with all the churches of Marion taking part, including a combined choir of more than a thousand, which she conducted. She was a charmer, or as my friend Else Blangstad, a film music editor, once said about her, "She's the kind of person when she's in the room, everybody else goes out of focus."

Dick's father, Merrill, was an orthopedic surgeon and the kind of small-town doctor everyone knows and admires. Boo and Merrill were very active in the Alumni Association of Indiana University, he was on the Board of Trustees, and they went to all the football games. Merrill was a former quarterback and liked to remind people "our goal line was never crossed." They quickly embraced my son and also Bob Carroll Jr., who used to play duets with Boo on the piano.

On our honeymoon, Dick told me to enjoy myself because it would probably be a long time before we were so totally alone again. I should have listened to the doctor.

To begin with, I was something of a novelty to his children. I came complete with several hundred *I Love Lucy* films, an autographed picture of Lucille Ball, and a writing partner with a beard. At one point, I had to squelch a plan to sell tickets to see me.

When we were first married, our group of small natives was very restless. Especially at night. They really hated to see that evening sun go down, and my little transplant from California was the most restless gun of all. Apparently, the only cure for this uneasy feeling was to climb into bed with Mommy and Daddy. Now, I can't honestly say I wasn't properly warned about this. When my furniture arrived, six-year-old Ned watched them bring in the king-sized mattress with amazement. "Hey," he said with anticipation, "how many people does that bed hold?" As it turned out, quite a few. I have heard of a ménage à trois, but ours was more of a ménage à quatre or sometimes cinq. Brian, being a teenager, stayed in his own room. Sharing the bed with assorted small folks got old pretty fast, so we made the bed off-limits. Our house had radiant heat in the floor and the rug was very toasty, so the accepted pattern was for each person to bring his blanket and pillow and find a place on the floor, with the first guy getting the choice locations next to the bed.

Now, we understood that the children were going through a period of adjustment, and the changes in personnel on the executive level had caused a rash of security blankets and thumb sucking. We understood the need for togetherness, and this made us more tolerant of our wall-to-wall children. It wasn't that we minded the company, but it was a little unnerving not to know if we were alone or not. I remember one particular time when Dick was kissing me good morning—you know how newlyweds are—and a small voice piped up from the floor, "Ah-ah-ah! No romancing in bed!"

And there was another occasion when Dick was on call at the hospital, the phone rang all night long, and small folks came and went from our bedroom as if it were a youth hostel. The last call came from the hospital at 4:30 A.M., Dick started to get dressed for the third time, and Michael, who I didn't even know was in the room, called out, "Hey, Mommy, your husband has to go out again!"

One night, when we had a particularly big turnout, I was climbing out of bed to do something—probably to check on what was the lawful capacity for a 15' x 15' bedroom, and Dick warned me, "Don't step on the children!"

Not only did I have to get adjusted to what my friend, Arthur Hamilton, the composer, called "my cast of thousands," but I had to get used to driving them everywhere, often in the snow. It doesn't snow too much in Los Angeles, and I got stuck in my own driveway three times before I mastered it. Then, too, I had to get used to living in a house that was built for Dick and his wife by the renowned architect Frank Lloyd Wright, or as one resident called it, "the funniest-looking house in town." To begin with, the house was built on a hexagon principle. All the walls were built at angles, coming off the side of the hexagon. The chimney in the middle of the living room was forty-two feet high, and the living room ceiling was twenty-eight feet high, and there were two wings going off from the sides. Mr. Wright said when the lights were on, he wanted the effect of a Chinese lantern. The first time I saw the house was at night, and he was right. It was lovely. But have you ever lived in a lantern?

As any fan of Mr. Wright's knows, he was fond of making his interiors like the inside of a ship, with lots of wood and cabinets so there wouldn't be so much clutter. He was also fond of long, narrow halls like gangways and small bedrooms. Not to mention small kitchens. Mr. Wright thought the kitchen should be accessible to the rest of the house and boy,

Brian, Michael, Dr. Richard Davis, Lisa, Ned, Madelyn and Charlotte in the living room of their Frank Lloyd Wright house in Marion, Indiana.

was it accessible! Children were drawn to it, sometimes from miles away, so they could squeeze past me when I was doing something at the stove. To be absolutely fair, I should add here that the kitchen was supposed to be three feet wider, but the contractor goofed. He also quit, and from then on, Dick became his own contractor and got his instructions from Mr. Wright on a phone hanging on a nearby tree. I secretly suspect that Mr. Wright had never cooked a meal in his life and didn't care much about kitchens.

I can tell you he never wore makeup, either. Due to the house's design, the living room was gorgeous and filled with light, but our bedroom and bath were built into the side of a small hill, and with the overhanging roof, it made them both very dark. When Dick shaved in the morning, there was a small chipmunk who used to sit on the rock wall outside the window and watch him. Sometimes when I was putting on makeup in the bathroom mirror, I could tell the chipmunk was thinking "too much eye shadow."

Living in a Frank Lloyd Wright house did have advantages, though. For one thing you met a lot of people. Sometimes total strangers drove up, chortling, "Is this really a house?" They had thought perhaps a restaurant, or at least a filling station. Then we got visiting young architects who wanted to see the house and worship at the shrine. Never mind that the lady of the shrine was in the shower washing her hair. And then there were the workmen. One workman's first remark on seeing the house was "Geez!" and his second remark was "What was Lucille Ball really like?" (He didn't read Hedda Hopper, but there are no secrets in a small town.) And what was I to tell the carpenter, that Lucille Ball was a delightful person and probably the funniest woman in the world, but when she doesn't think the script is good enough, she reacts much the same way as he does when he hits his thumb with the hammer?

I finally learned to appreciate the house. And honestly, I am not just saying this because it is now in the National Registry of Historic Houses, and I am trying not to look like a clod. It was rather like the way one feels about an eccentric friend. After you learned to accept that the house was different from other houses, you loved it for that difference. I finally told Dick that I loved the house, but that I really loathed it at first. And of course, he just looked at me, smiled and said, "I know you did."

In between driving children to music lessons and Girl Scout meetings, getting stuck in the driveway in the snow, and discussing makeup with a chipmunk, I also was trying to write with my partner. Bob was good enough to drive my car back to Indiana and became a frequent visitor. Later, Dick's cousin George, who owned the local airport, used to fly up to Chicago and meet Bob and fly him back down so we

Bob Carroll Jr. visited Marion, Indiana, so often to write with Madelyn that the Holiday Inn put up a sign.

could work. Bob stayed at the local Holiday Inn so often that one time when he came back to Marion, the hotel put up a sign on the marquee "Welcome home Robert Carroll Jr." A religious group had put signs along the highway outside of town that said, "Where will you spend eternity?" and Bob remarked, "At the Holiday Inn." We wrote two specials for Dinah Shore and a movie. On his own, Bob did a rewrite on a movie for Doris Day called *Do Not Disturb,* which he said should have been called *Do Not Distribute.*

One time, when Bob was visiting Marion in the spring of 1965, we had a tornado, which cut across the state and caused devastation in the south part of town. We had no electricity for forty-eight hours, and since we had an electric stove, this was tricky. My housekeeper Lu Gulley, who came with me from Los Angeles, solved the problem by emptying the freezer and cooking in the 6' x 8' fireplace, which I'm sure would have made Mr. Wright proud. Lu said her grandmother taught her to cook over an open fire in Tupelo, Mississippi.

Again, Hedda Hopper found all this worthy of an item. She wrote in her column:

> "Bob Carroll went to Marion, Indiana, to confer with his collaborator Madelyn Martin Davis (they did the *I Love Lucy* show) on *Fifth Avenue Folly*, which they're writing for Twentieth Century-Fox. He arrived just as the tornado struck. He wrote, 'It went right by us and we had a forty-eight-hour telephone blackout and no electricity. Following the wind, it became black as night, then hail the size of golf balls engulfed the area.' For three days and nights, Bob and Madelyn helped her husband Dr. Richard Davis as he tended the wounded."

I was not too sure about Hedda's sources. Dick was at the hospital for two days straight, but I assure you he didn't ask two comedy writers to scrub up and assist him in the ER.

SIXTEEN

Who Am I?

AFTER WE HAD LIVED IN INDIANA ALMOST TWO YEARS, we decided to move the family to Los Angeles. Desi heard the news from our mutual agent Marvin Moss and phoned Dick. "Doc, I hear you're moving back. Is it okay with you if Mallen goes back to work?" I guess somewhere in Desi's background was that Latin patriarch who consults another male head of a family about the plans for the women folk. But I was too pleased at already being offered a writing job so soon to be offended. Dick told him he'd better talk to me. He did, and explained he wanted Bob and me to create some sitcoms for his new company, Desi Arnaz Productions.

We were worried about uprooting the children, but they handled it well and were excited about the idea of moving to California. The only one who didn't go for it was my son Michael, who I thought would be thrilled. And even though

I explained we were moving back to his old neighborhood, he was unenthusiastic about making another change.

We set out across the country in two cars, Dick and I and the three youngest children in the station wagon, and Brian driving my car with Charlotte. It was a fairly uneventful trip, and we were only asked "are we there yet?" twenty-seven times. As we drove up in front of our new house in West Los Angeles, the moving van was parked at the curb waiting for us. While I was telling the men where to put all the boxes, the phone rang. It was Desi, suggesting that I come to the Desilu Culver Studios, where he had set up shop, and pick out the furniture for our new office. He explained I could just drive down Overland Avenue to Culver City, like it was right next door. This was pretty much the way things went from then on. It wasn't long before I was writing a weekly TV comedy and running a household of seven people (three of them teenagers, which counts as two each) and longing for the good old days when all I had to worry about was a tornado.

When people discuss today's women who try to hold down a job, be a good wife and a responsible, caring mother, they don't talk too much about the "G" factor, as in "guilt." I saw Jamie Lee Curtis on a talk show once, and she spoke about how she tells her child, "Mommy has to go to work." She explained that it would be more honest to say, "Mommy wants to go to work." What she was admitting was that it is more fun to hang from a helicopter with Arnold Schwarzenegger or watch Lucille Ball stamp grapes than to be a driver in the mommy carpool or a den mother for the Cub Scouts. So you have this little voice in your head that is nattering away and saying you're not being a good mother. For instance, you should be there when they come home from school, and the children shouldn't always be with a housekeeper or in daycare, right?

The family returns to Los Angeles and moves into a house in Westwood.

The trouble is when I made a point of being home at that all-important moment in the afternoon, they buried themselves in cartoons on TV, talked on the phone for an hour to the boyfriends they had just left at school, or went into their rooms and slammed the door, intimating there was some crisis you would just as soon not know about. Or, in Ned's case, went running down the street to practice in a neighbor's garage with his band. The other members of the band were Marc and Joseph Williams, sons of the composer-conductor John Williams, and they called their group "The Communist Toothbrush."

So it's hard to know how to play it. I tried to be home for dinner every night, even if I had to go back to the studio, so we could all be together at the end of the day. You know, having stimulating conversations about activities and sharing thoughts. Well, the only trouble with that was, when you said, "How was school today?," they said, "Sickening!" and the repartee went downhill from there. The conversation was something like this:

US:

"Would anyone like to talk about what happened in the news today?"

"You're getting the ends of your hair in your food."

"Where is your napkin?"

"What if we all spoke French at dinner?"

"Tomatoes do not make you gag."

THEM:

"Euugh! What's that icky stuff on my plate?"

"I sat on my retainer, but it's only a little broken."

"Who invented turnips anyway?"

"I'm eating left handed because I got a blister on my right thumb from snapping my fingers when I danced The Jerk."

"There's a funny smell in my room. Do you think it's that dead bird I have in a shoe box?"

Then Michael threw up the tomatoes, and I went back to the studio.

The trouble with being a working mother is that you develop multiple personalities. You know who you are, you just don't know who you are *when*. I have these different roles, mother, doctor's wife, and sitcom writer, and sometimes I play the wrong role in the wrong scene. Charlotte was once giving me some lame excuse why she was out past curfew, and I heard myself saying, "You need a better punch line." One noon I was standing in line to pay my check at the Universal Studios commissary, and I was behind Joe Namath, the football star. He was very muscled about his shoulders, and it gave him the appearance of bad posture. To my horror, I heard myself saying, "Stand up straight, dear." Fortunately, he didn't hear me, or pretended not to hear me, thinking I was a crazed fan.

My friend, Ann Powelson Smith, who is a lawyer and had seven children, told me she was at a dinner party one night, sitting next to Steve McQueen, and she looked at his plate and exclaimed, "You haven't touched your vegetables!"

While I lived in Marion, Bob and I wrote some scripts, but it was on my own timetable, so I had not actually been in the combat zone known as sitcom writing since I had acquired a large family. In the first year when I moved back to Los Angeles, Bob and I created three pilots and worked on *The Mothers-in-Law* for Desi's company. Two of the pilots didn't sell, but *The Mothers-in-Law* did. This was a show in which two couples live side by side. They are very different, but they have to tolerate each other because their kids get married. Eve Arden played the upscale mother of the bride (Debbie Walley), and Herb Rudley played her lawyer husband. Kaye Ballard was the volatile Italian mother of the groom (Jerry Fogel), and her husband, a writer, was played first by Roger Carmel and then by Richard Deacon. They were all wonderful performers. Bob and I had a great time doing married humor along with the dynamics of two generations trying to get along in the situations that come up with in-laws who unfortunately lived next door to each other, while their kids were living in the converted garage.

It was good to be working with Desi again, with his enthusiasm for the projects we were doing together and his support for writers. I remember we turned in one script, and the account executive at the advertising agency didn't like it. In those days, the agency played a major role in the process. Each program would have one sponsor instead of multiples, and the agency functioned much like the networks do today. The ad executive called us and told us that the script wasn't

Madelyn, Eve Arden, Kaye Ballard, and Bob Carroll Jr. backstage at The Mothers-in-Law.

funny. I asked Desi if we should throw it out or rewrite or what. He said, "I'll take care of it." Word came back that the script was fine, and we were going ahead with it as is. I didn't hear what happened until weeks later. Desi had called up the executive and said, "Don't you ever call my writers like that again. If you have a problem, call me, and I'll deal with it." The exec was quite cool to us from then on, but we didn't have to do a big rewrite! And, oh yes, the show turned out to be one of our best and was very funny.

One of the better shows we did in that series came from an idea given to us by Kaye Ballard. She said her sister-in-law asked her husband one of those hypothetical questions women ask when they should know better. She asked, "If I weren't home and Elizabeth Taylor's car broke down in front of our house, and she came in to use the phone, would you take her out to dinner?" Kaye's brother made the mistake of saying yes. We made this into a show in which Eve and Kaye both ask their husbands the same question and are given the same wrong answers with the predictable results.

Another episode I was fond of was "Didn't You Used to Be Ossie Snick?" It starred Ozzie Nelson and was written by Fred S. Fox and Seaman Jacobs. Kaye had exaggerated and said she used to sing with Ossie Snick's band, and when he came to town and Eve wanted to meet him, she was in trouble. Ozzie was a lot of fun to work with and composed an original song for the show called "North Dakota Moon," a takeoff on the romantic ballads of the '40s. He was an individualist and an athlete, and people thought he was eccentric because in the days before it was so popular, he used to jog every morning from his house above Hollywood Boulevard to the studio where they filmed *Ozzie and Harriet*, take a shower and go to work.

We never did a show with Harriet Nelson, but we became friends with them both. One time, when they were at our house for dinner, she was wearing a new sable jacket that Ozzie had given her for Christmas. Harriet, who started out as a singer with Ozzie's band long before, proudly said that the jacket was for thirty years of service.

One day Kaye Ballard announced that she was bringing Bea Lillie to my house for dinner the next Sunday, and she would bring the dinner. Bea was the famous British musical comedy star, who was visiting in the United States. I was delighted to know I was going to meet her, but I didn't have any help on Sunday, and suddenly I was giving a dinner party for Kaye, Bea Lillie, her manager, Bob Carroll, and the hilarious comic Paul Lynde, one of Kaye's best friends. I solved the problem by paying the kids to help. Lisa and Charlotte would do the dishes and Brian, who was good at such things, would serve.

Everything went smoothly, and after dinner we went into the living room and all got down on the rug and played a form of lawn bowling, a game that Bob had brought. Brian joined us in playing the game, and Bea remarked to someone that it was all so democratic for us to let the servants join in the game, and she loved American customs.

For the first season of *The Mothers-in-Law,* Bob and I wrote fourteen of the twenty-six shows and supervised the writing of the others. There were rehearsals and weekend rewrites and all the usual stuff. Before I start applying for the title of Wonder Woman, I must add that I didn't have to do laundry, clean the house, or make the meals since I had a live-in housekeeper (the one who went back to Marion with me and who cooked in the fireplace when the electricity went out because of the tornado). She had recently married, but she agreed to come back to work for us. I was amazed she would agree to live in four nights a week. She was not only a great cook but a philosopher. She told me, "Every marriage needs a little airin' out."

If you plan to supervise the lives of five children and write a weekly TV show, it is a good idea to have a supportive husband. Dick was great at filling in, taking the children to music lessons, art lessons, orthodontist appointments, and to the snow near Gorman, California, to go sledding because Mom was doing a last-minute rewrite. Of course, it was also fortuitous that he was a doctor because he was quick to know if it was a real sore throat or a "I goofed and didn't finish my project for Social Studies so I don't want to go to school" throat. And he really came in handy in the middle of the night when I could just poke him and say, "He's throwing up again." Doctors don't mind that kind of thing at all. This made it so I didn't have to feel guilty if I had a sick child and a sick script that needed fixing all at the same time because Doc was in charge of the situation.

Dick came to every show I wrote and sat in the audience, sometimes bringing the children. If someone in the cast suddenly became ill, the assistant director never had to come out and ask, "Is there a doctor in the house?" because he knew there was. One night during the filming of *The Mothers-in-Law,* Eve Arden fainted backstage, and Dick came to the rescue. Kaye Ballard used him as a consultant for all her actor friends, and when she was one of the TV commentators for the Rose Parade, she said hello to Dr. Richard Davis or, as she called him, "Doctor to the stars."

I think it was about this time when old Mom seemed to be spreading herself a little thin and started developing what Dick says in medical terms is "The Tired Mother Syndrome." I remember one night I was getting pretty testy about something and Michael explained, "Well, Mommy, you can't win 'em all!" I was getting the feeling I couldn't win 'em any. When this sort of thing happened, Dick would usually say that we had to get away. So we would plan to get a sitter and go somewhere over the weekend, just the two of us. Our wanting to go away by ourselves puzzled young Ned. "Why are you going away without us?" he wanted to know. I tried to put it diplomatically that I seemed to need a rest, but he didn't get it. Finally, I told him bluntly we were going away to get away from all of them. "Come on," he said, "why are you *really* going?"

Whenever we went out of town, Desi invariably called. He said he wanted to be sure I was getting enough rest, but he also liked to talk about some of the projects he was considering. He asked Bob's and my advice often. It wasn't that our opinions were so valuable, but I think he knew we would tell him the truth. If a pilot idea sounded like a bomb, we would say so. Some people don't like to tell the boss the truth because, with good reason, they're afraid of being fired. I guess we weren't afraid of that, or maybe it was because my mother instilled in me, "Always tell the truth, and you won't get into trouble."

Weekends away helped some, but I kept having this irresistible urge to go out and sit in the car and have a good cry, or go into the closet and shut the door.

One night we were invited to Ken Murray's house. Ken was a former vaudevillian and comedian who owned the *Black-Outs*, a stage show which consisted of novelty acts and vaudeville sketches and ran for over seven years in the El Capitan Theater on Vine Street in Hollywood. He and his wife invited us, along with Lucy, Desi, and some others, to have dinner, and the entertainment afterward was home movies that Ken always took at Hollywood gatherings at homes of stars. During the showing of the movies, I was sitting near Ken as he ran the projector, and I don't know if it was the nearness to the huge cigar he always smoked or what, but when the lights were turned on, everybody got up to leave, and I was afraid to stand up because I knew I was going to faint. I tried to hold things together until we could reach the car, but I didn't make it. So there I was, stretched out on the couch while the room went round and round, feeling very queasy. Desi's reaction was to say accusingly, "Are you pregnant again?" Somehow, Dick managed to get me home and put me to bed. I slept solidly for fifteen hours and when I got up, I felt fine.

During the second season of *The Mothers-in-Law,* Desi called Dick in the middle of the night, telling him not to wake me up but to give me his news in the morning, like I slept in my own suite down the hall. The news was that he had diverticulitis and was leaving for the hospital to be operated on. Elliott Lewis took over as producer. The series was great fun to work on, but despite all our efforts, it ended after the second season.

Bob and I worked for a brief time on *The Debbie Reynolds Show,* writing or overseeing the last six shows of the season. Jess Oppenheimer was leaving the show, which had some problems, and asked us to fill in. At that particular time, Michael and Ned were taking some summer classes at a private school, and one of their classmates was Bill Allen, Steve Allen and Jayne Meadows's son. I ran into Jayne at a party, and she couldn't wait to tell me the conversation our kids had. She said they were discussing who their parents were, and Bill said his father was the comic Steve Allen, and Michael announced his mother was a writer and right now she was saving *The Debbie Reynolds Show.* Obviously, I didn't.

We were taking a short hiatus from work when Lucille Ball called. Dick answered the phone and she told him, "I need to talk to Madelyn and tell her to get a chair because this is going to be a long conversation." She was starring in the *Here's Lucy* series at the time. She explained to me how she had dinner with Richard Burton and Elizabeth Taylor, and they had told her they would love to guest on her show. Since they were the hottest celebrity couple in the country at that time, she was very excited about it and wanted Bob and me to write the script, which sounded great to me. No problem. Well, there was a little problem. They needed the script in five days. We managed to do it and started working for Lucy again, writing a third of the scripts for each of the next three seasons.

"Lucy Meets the Burtons" opened the 1970-71 season of *Here's Lucy.* The story centered around the enormous diamond ring that Burton had recently given his wife. Burton shows it to Lucy, and she insists on trying it on and (what else?) gets it stuck on her finger. When I checked the facts lately, I read that the ring was 69 carats. I thought maybe this was one of those stories that gets told so often it becomes fact. My memory was that it was about 35 carats, which is still huge. I checked with my friend, Nan Birmingham, who writes about gems, and she confirmed that, according to the Diamond

Elizabeth Taylor, Lucy, Richard Burton, and "the ring" appear on Here's Lucy.

Directory of America, the stone was indeed 69.42 carats. I'm surprised Liz could lift her arm. If you care to keep track of these things, it was sold, but is still called the Taylor-Burton diamond and was last reported to be in Saudi Arabia.

It was great fun to work with Lucy again, and we felt as if we were back home. Nothing seemed to have changed because during rehearsal, she came to me in the bleachers, and we had another one of our little girl-talks. Since Richard Burton was originally a stage actor, he was rehearsing by just walking around the set and saying his lines quietly to get the general feel of the scene, not thinking it was necessary to give a full-out reading. Now, Lucy liked to rehearse as if each time was a performance, so Burton was driving her crazy.

She gave me my orders, "You've got to tell Richard Burton to speak up." This was a tough one. In the first place, this was the director's job. And secondly, what was I going to say to one of the world's finest Shakespearean actors, "Listen, Dick, would you please speak up and stop mumbling?" I took the only way out and did nothing. Lucy never mentioned it again and, of course, on the show, in front of the audience, Burton did speak up with great authority, and Lucy was thrilled with his performance. Afterwards, she complimented him, saying, "You were fantastic! You got fourteen laughs!" Burton quietly corrected her. "Sixteen," he said.

I had another little chat, prior to rehearsal, only this time it was with the director, Jerry Paris. Jerry was very experienced, having directed *The Dick Van Dyke Show, Happy Days* and *The Odd Couple,* and was doing a fine job of handling three superstars, but he had an assignment for me. At the time of the show, Elizabeth Taylor was recovering from an illness, and since most of the scenes revolved around Burton, she wasn't coming in until the last two days of rehearsal. Lucy, who was concerned about Burton's line delivery, had been giving him quite a bit of direction. Jerry said to me, "You have to tell Lucy that Richard Burton says if she treats Elizabeth the way she has been treating him, Elizabeth will walk out." This was one I didn't think I could ignore, so I repeated the conversation to Gary Morton, Lucy's husband and the show's executive producer. He told me, "I'll talk to her." Later, when Miss Taylor arrived, things went swimmingly, and I asked Gary how he had managed it. He said, "I told Lucy that Elizabeth had been very sick, her health was precarious, and we had to treat her carefully." This, of course, brought out all of Lucy's legendary maternal qualities, and she handled Miss Taylor as if she were made of glass and never uttered a cross word.

After the performance, there was a party on the set for

the cast and crew and the celebrities in the audience. I wanted to thank the Burtons, so I found Miss Taylor, told her how wonderful she was in the show, and introduced her to my husband Dick. "Do you want to see the ring?" she asked. Well, of course, we were dying to but didn't want to seem crass by saying so. I hadn't actually seen the real ring since it was only used on camera, and the minute the scene was over, a security guard whisked it away somewhere. A fake was used during rehearsal and copies were given out as souvenirs. So, Miss Taylor rubbed the ring on a near-by tablecloth and held out her hand for inspection. The ring was beautifully cut and absolutely gorgeous. Secretly, I had thought, "Who would want such a thing?" Well, to name one, me.

Next, I turned to Richard Burton and thanked him for his terrific performance. And what did he answer? "But you wrote it, luv." Somehow after that, Richard Burton became my favorite guest star.

While we were writing for *Here's Lucy*, we were having our usual "what'll-we-write-this-week?" discussion when Bob looked up at a poster on the wall that featured a penguin. "We've never had her be a penguin," he said. So we wrote a script called "The Franchise Fiasco" in which Lucy decides to make money by investing in a franchise frozen custard place called "The Proud Penguin." Business is so bad she is forced to advertise by walking around town in a penguin costume with a sign on her back and, as luck would have it, some real penguins have escaped from the zoo, and they insist on following her. Everything was fine, and Lucy didn't mind working with penguins, but the penguin wranglers hadn't bothered to tell us that this was molting season and when they are molting, the birds get quite cranky and don't want to do anything but stand around and sulk about how moth-eaten they look. They finally followed her, but they were muttering under their beaks.

Another script we did for this series was lifted from my husband Dick's family history. For some reason, a branch of his mother's family, starting with his great uncle, Ben, named all their children Ben and Fred. They were doctors, lawyers, and judges and perfectly capable of making other choices, but they seemed fixated on the same names. It made it very difficult to identify people so someone would know who you were talking about. You would have to say, "Ben's Ben" or "Ben's Ben's Fred" and that sort of thing. In "Lucy's Last Blind Date," the wonderful Don Knotts played Lucy's date who was visiting from Indiana and falls in love with her and wants to marry her. He won't take no for an answer, so to discourage him she tells him her family is a little odd. He says that's okay, his family is a little peculiar, too. They give everybody the same names. He explains:

BEN

For some reason, my family is stuck on certain names. You see, originally my grandfather Ben was one of two brothers. The other brother was named Fred. Then Ben had two sons and he named them Ben and Fred. Meanwhile, Fred had two sons and he named them Fred and Ben. So everybody got to referring to them as Ben's Ben and Ben's Fred, or Fred's Ben and Fred's Fred. Then when Ben's Ben got married...that was my father... he named me Ben and my brother Fred. Then, my uncle Fred got married, and he named two of his sons Fred and Ben. So in order to know who you were talking about, you'd have to say Ben's Fred's Ben or Ben's Fred's Fred. Meanwhile, just to make matters worse, Uncle Fred had a daughter and he named her Gayle, after my mother named Gayle. So it became Fred's Gayle or Ben's Gayle. Then Fred's Gayle had a daughter and she named her Gayle.

Desi Arnaz, Jr., Gale Gordon, and Lucie Arnaz appear with Lucy on Here's Lucy.

> Then, of course, you had to say whether you meant Ben's Gayle or Fred's Gayle's Gayle... Well, we kind of got used to it, but one year a census taker came to town and after an hour and a half, her hair turned snow white, and she went streaking out of town!

So we exaggerated a little, but not much. My husband's second cousin Ben is a retired surgeon and a noted sculptor. He and his wife Nancy are good friends of ours, but he really is Ben's Ben's Ben.

One time I was on a plane from Los Angeles to Indianapolis and happened to sit next to Tom Harmon, the legendary football star of the University of Michigan, newscaster, and father of Mark Harmon. We were having a nice chat, and I told him we were related by marriage. I explained that my husband's mother was first cousin to his brother Harold's wife Gayle, whose mother was also named Gayle, so she was known in the family as Gayle's Gayle, not to be confused with my husband's mother's other cousin Ben's Ben, whose wife was known as Ben's Ben's Gayle. It wasn't long before Tom said he had work to do and moved to another seat.

In another episode, "Lucy and Her All-Nun Band," the idea actually came from just that—an all-nun band. Dick was on the staff at St. John's Hospital in Santa Monica, California, and they were having their annual Christmas party, with music provided by a band composed of nuns from The Sisters of Charity from Leavenworth, Kansas. As soon as they took a break, I approached the leader and asked if they would be allowed to play on television. "You bet!" she said, and we used the actual band in the show. In the script, the saxophone player got the flu and so Guess Who put on a nun's outfit and sat in with the band. Mary Wickes played the bass and Freddy Martin, a saxophone-playing orchestra leader from the Big Band era, played himself and gave Lucy a lesson on the sax.

Being married to a doctor came in handy again when Lucy took up skiing at the age of 60. She and her husband Gary Morton were at our house for dinner one night, and they were going to Snow Mass, Colorado, the next morning. My husband, who had done a lot of orthopedic work as a general surgeon, warned her jovially as they were leaving to be careful and not break her leg. And of course, she did. When a star in a series has an accident, your first thought (at least I hope it is your first thought) is for her well-being. Your very next thought is, "Geez, what do we do now?" There was a lot of scrambling around and shelving of scripts, and the writers began to think of shows we could do where Lucy wouldn't have to move. This wasn't easy since her physical gags were the highlight of the show. Bob and I conferred with Dick about things like casts and fusions and fibulas and tibias.

We wrote one episode in which Lucy is in a hospital bed and Eva Gabor was her roommate. In another, Lloyd Bridges played her doctor, and in one called "Harrison Carter, Male Nurse," Lucy came home from the hospital and had Gale Gordon take care of her, the demanding invalid.

I don't think we even discussed shutting down the show. Lucy wouldn't hear of it. As she said, "Why would you shut down the show when I could do it with my leg in a cast?"

SEVENTEEN

Who's the Pushy Broad at the End of the Table?

When I made my first trip to Europe just before *I Love Lucy* began, I remember thinking I'd better see every city and museum and art gallery on the whole continent just in case I never came back again. I wasn't far wrong, as my next trip was twenty-six years later in 1977 when Dick and I took a five-week trip to London, Paris, and Rome. Dick the surgeon had never taken more than a week's vacation in his whole life and couldn't believe he was doing it. I think he thought people were going to come hobbling after him, dragging their crutches and holding their gall bladders, moaning, "How can you take a vacation when I need you?"

Bob Carroll Jr. kept an eye on the kids. The only ones still at home were Ned and Michael, who were attending UCLA. I was looking forward to the trip, but was a little apprehensive because Dick is an art, architecture, and history enthusiast, and I was afraid I would never get him out of the museums and galleries. I am the kind of art lover who whips through galleries and is waiting for my friends in the lobby, tapping my foot. But Dick behaved very reasonably, although I had a feeling he really would have liked to stay all night in the Louvre.

On one of our excursions, we were in the St. Pietro in Vincoli church in Rome, to see Michaelangelo's statue of Moses, and I stayed long enough to hear a lady in the crowd say with delight, "He *does* look like Charlton Heston!' We had a terrific time, returning on the QE2. Bob and I went directly into writing and producing one of the Lucille Ball specials *Lucy Calls the President.* This was based on the custom of President Jimmy Carter dropping by to visit ordinary citizens, and Lucy thinks he is coming to their house. Guesting in the show were Vivian Vance, Ed McMahon, who played Lucy's husband, Steve Allen, Mary Jane Croft, Mary Wickes, and Gale Gordon, with a phone call from Lillian Carter, the President's mother.

After the audience filed in and a welcoming speech by Gary Morton, Lucy was scheduled to make her entrance. There was a long, awkward pause. She finally appeared, and the reason she had a problem coming out was that her mother had died recently and part of her routine was always to introduce her mother in the stands. This was the first time she had ever done a show when her mother wasn't in the audience.

While we were rehearsing Lucy's special on the Warner Bros. lot, Bob and I had a call to come to the office of Alan Shayne, WB head of television, to have a meeting with him and Tony Barr of CBS. They were looking for new producers on the sitcom *Alice,* which took place in Mel's Diner. It starred the talented Linda Lavin with a great supporting cast of Polly Holliday, Vic Tayback, Beth Howland, and Philip McKeon as Alice's son. The show had already been on the air one year. Apparently, we made a good impression, or maybe we were handy, because we were hired. It turned out we were not only hired, but were to report the day after we finished the special. The reason for the haste was there were problems (aren't there always on new sitcoms?).

Fortunately, we didn't find out right away that we were the fifth set of producers in one year. They were already in production, and we discovered they had taped four shows they weren't too crazy about, had one script ahead, and were going on the air in five weeks. I mean, Bob and I like a challenge, but not quite that much of a challenge. So we started scrambling and working weekends, trying to pull things together. We assembled a writing staff over the years that included Arthur Marx and Bob Fisher, Vic Rauseo and Linda Morris, Mark Egan and Mark Soloman, Gail Honingberg, Charles Isaacs, Bob and Howard Bendetson, David Silverman and Stephen Sustarsic, and Sandy Krinski and Chet Dowling. The crew was already in place and pretending not to notice that most of our expertise was in three-camera film and not tape.

Early on, the charming and gentlemanly Alan Shayne turned out to be a mentor for us, like Desi. We sent one of our first scripts to CBS for approval, and word came back from the network executive that he didn't much care for it. I called Alan and told him the bad news and asked him what to do now. I thought perhaps the show would soon have a fifth set of producers who left. He said, "Do you and Bob think it's good?" and I said, "Yes," and he said he would get back to me, and he did. The script was in, and it turned out to be a very good show. It is a little-known secret that writers do their best work if you just let them write and don't have twelve people telling them how to fix the script. If Shakespeare were writing for TV, I can hear the executive's advice now. "Bill, I think you ought to lose the balcony scene." Later, Chuck Schnebel and Dwayne Hickman (of *Dobie Gillis* fame)

Vic Tayback (Mel), Philip McKeon (Tommy), Polly Holliday (Flo), Linda Lavin (Alice), and Beth Howland (Vera) starred in Alice.

were our CBS contacts, and they were very supportive. If someone wanted us to do something we didn't want to do, we would say, "The network doesn't like it" and they would back us up. We produced the show for eight years.

By now the network's department of Standards and Practices had loosened up a little. You were allowed "three hells and a damn" to be sprinkled through each show, if you really needed them, which was a giant step from the days when we couldn't even say "pregnant." One of our friends was in the censorship department, and he had the tough job of going to the set to inspect if there was too much cleavage.

For directors, we turned to Marc Daniels, who had worked with us on *I Love Lucy.* Marc came into our office carrying the first script he was going to direct and announced he had a few little changes he wanted to make. My heart sank as I envisioned a big rewrite because I remembered he was very meticulous, maybe even picky. His first big change was in the second scene in the diner. He said, "Flo serves the customer, and then one page later, the customer gets up, pays his bill, and leaves. He hasn't had time to eat his breakfast." He had other monumental changes like that. He became our main director, and we saved our most difficult shows for him, like having a tree fall through the roof of the diner or driving a truck through the front door. We became best friends, and he ended up directing ninety episodes of the series.

Incidentally, the show in which we crashed the truck into the diner, written by Vic Rauseo and Linda Morris (who later won Emmys for *Frasier*), almost got me into trouble. The truck was to be driven by Flo with Alice and Vera in the front seat with her. Polly practiced driving the truck around the Warner's lot, and Jerry Madden, our line producer, had a special break-away wall made for the front of the diner. Linda Lavin was a little nervous about doing the stunt and wasn't sure she wanted to go hurtling through a wall, break-away or not. I was so used to trying things out for Lucy, I heard myself saying, "I'll do it." Not being a stunt woman or an actress, I don't know what possessed me to think I should put on a pink uniform and pretend to be Alice. Luckily, Linda wasn't about to be upstaged by her executive producer, so she quickly agreed to do it. The stunt worked beautifully, the truck came crashing through the front wall of the diner, the audience screamed with laughter and disbelief, and Polly stopped at exactly the place she was supposed to. If she hadn't, she might have demolished the whole diner set, not to mention Vic Tayback, who was standing behind the counter.

I must admit I felt some prejudice against me when I became a producer. There was a tendency to regard me as invisible and ignore me like the invisible woman comedy writers of years before. There is still a lingering perception that if you're a man and you give your opinion, you're forceful. If you're a woman and you give the same opinion, you're domineering. One director referred to me as a "real bossy dame." Another critique came from an actor during a reading of an *Alice* script. He was sitting down at one end of the table, and I was at the other. He asked the person next to him, "Who's the pushy broad at the end of the table who's doing all the yakking?" Now, word travels at a studio so fast it makes the speed of light seem pokey, so of course I was immediately told. They say, "Living well is the best revenge." Not really. Not ever hiring actors again who say things like that is.

Executive producers or "show runners" of sitcoms, women or men, are usually writers. They are the ones who can ultimately come up with that script every week. They also hire directors, audition actors, oversee postproduction, and are responsible for the whole show running smoothly. Their duties can be as varied as drying the tears of an actress who feels she has been insulted by the director, sympathizing with the director who feels the star is throwing her weight around, placating the star who feels that everyone is against him or her, and telling the studio and the network that this week things couldn't be better. One of the oddest jobs Bob and I ever had was to audition guard dogs. These were Dobermans, and their trainer had them snarl on cue and act fierce. The trainer assured us that they could look more menacing and showed us some sets of false teeth he had made for them that had longer fangs.

One of the duties that falls to producers besides hiring is firing. Nobody likes to do this, but when you look around, no one else is holding up his hand and volunteering. The buck stops you know where. We had hired an actor to play a supporting role on an episode of *Alice*. Word came to us from the set that he was dissatisfied with his part and was telling everyone he thought the script was lousy. When an actor doesn't like the script, it can spread like a virus, and soon all the other actors are complaining about the material and getting headaches and suggesting rewrites, so the man had to go. We called the casting director, and she said she would notify his agent and suggested a replacement, whom we hired. Unfortunately, the actor's agent didn't give him the bad news because of some glitch, and both actors showed up on the set the next morning. Don Corvan, the assistant director, called our office in alarm to report the problem. Now, the few times we had to fire somebody, Bob did it because he didn't hate it as much as I did. So it was my turn. I went to the set and learned that the doomed actor had gone out to repark his car, not dreaming he had been replaced. I waited by the door, thinking this way he could make a graceful exit without meeting anybody. On the other side of the flat in the Mel's Diner set, there was a deadly quiet. I really was sincerely sorry and hoped to get the whole thing over with quickly. The actor came in the door, I intercepted him, and our conversation went like this:

ME

Hi, we heard you were unhappy with your material, so you've been replaced. Your agent was supposed to tell you last night. I'm terribly sorry. I wouldn't have had this happen for the world.

ACTOR

But I don't understand. I've never been fired before.

ME

Well, I'm terribly sorry. I wouldn't have had this happen for the world.

ACTOR

But I've never been fired before.

ME

I'm terribly sorry. I wouldn't have had this happen for the world.

I thought maybe we were going to spend the rest of our lives saying the same thing back and forth to each other when a hand appeared from behind the flat. The hand was holding the actor's jacket, which he had left when he first came to the set. The actor took the jacket from the hand and headed out the door, saying:

ACTOR

But I've never been fired before.

ME

I'm terribly sorry. I wouldn't have had this happen for the world.

And he left.

Sometimes a producer has to be a good translator and figure out what the star is really saying:

"That beach scene isn't written well" means "I don't look good in a bathing suit."

"Throwing cake in someone's face is too slapstick." Translation: "I don't get to have cake thrown at me."

"This scene is just talk, talk, talk" means "I'm not in it."

"This scene doesn't work at all"—rough translation, "I don't have enough jokes."

By the end of the '50s, quite a few talented women were beginning to infiltrate the comedy writing ranks, and by the '70s and '80s there were lots of women producers and executive producers. When we were working on *Alice* for Warner Bros., I looked around one day and was really proud to see that on that particular week, there was a woman star, two supporting women actors, a woman guest star, a woman executive producer, a woman producer, four women writers

Producers Jerry Madden, Linda Lavin (Star), Madelyn Davis and Bob Carroll Jr. celebrate winning the Golden Globe Award for Best Situation Comedy in 1979.

on staff, a woman director, a woman assistant director, a woman cameraperson, and a woman carpenter. Is that reverse discrimination? I hope so.

On another occasion, I realized that there were five people from Indiana on the show. The production assistant was Chris Ballard from Indianapolis, as was Duane Campbell, who played a steady customer in the diner. Marc Summers, the warm-up man, was from Carmel, Indiana. Dave Madden, who had been a regular on *Laugh In* and *The Partridge Family,* was with us that week, and he was from Terre Haute. The guest star, Forrest Tucker, who played Flo's father, was from Plainfield, Indiana. It was a total coincidence, but Bob called it "The Attack of the Hoosiers" and there was a story in the *Indianapolis Star-News,* with that as a headline.

One morning I went to the office and was greeted by our secretary Kathy Rosenwink with the news, "You made the

National Enquirer!" This is the tabloid paper that is always digging up scandals about the stars. A few weeks before, we had received several letters criticizing the show, and they ended up on my desk. They were intelligently written, and their complaints had some validity, so I sat down one day and rattled off some answers. I did it first because I have always believed it's rude not to answer letters, and secondly because I thought it was good for public relations. A person may be disgruntled with a show, but they wouldn't mind telling their friends that they got a personal letter from the producer and that might keep them watching. A couple of weeks later, an item appeared in *The Enquirer* that said they had sent out two bogus letters, written by reporters, to the producers of twenty different TV series, suggesting how to improve the shows. The point *The Enquirer* hoped to make was that producers don't really care about audience complaints. Out of the twenty they wrote to, sixteen producers never bothered to answer. Three responded to one letter, but ignored the other. And only one, they said, Madelyn Davis, the producer of *Alice,* responded to both letters with a warm, personal note. How's that for a scandal!

We inherited some very good characters as the show was based on the movie *Alice Doesn't Live Here Anymore,* written by Robert Getchell. The regulars in the cast were not only talented but were disciplined, never late to the set, never missed a show because apparently they were never sick in all the time we worked with them. Vic Tayback developed a herniated disc in his back, was in pain, but did the show anyway, having a hospital bed brought into his dressing room so he could lie down between scenes, and leaned against the counter a lot. Polly Holliday left to do her own series *Flo* and was replaced by Diane Ladd, who was the original *Flo* in the movie. And when she left, the part was played by Broadway actress Celia Weston.

The marvelously funny Martha Raye played Mel's mother. We hired her for one particular episode, and she was so great, we eventually brought her back for twelve more shows, including one where we could feature her fine jazz singing. She wasn't really old enough to be Mel's mother, so the first time she was to appear we discussed how to age her. I suggested perhaps she might wear some little glasses. "Oh, no, honey," she said, "I wouldn't want to hide my eyes." She was absolutely right, of course. The eyes are everything in comedy, and this veteran comic knew it. (If you doubt it, watch Lucy's eyes sometime.) Martha was the only comic I ever saw do a double take with her back to the camera and get a laugh.

We had some other fine guests on the show from time to time, including Eve Arden, Florence Henderson, Joel Grey, Robert Goulet, and the inimitable Art Carney. One of my favorite episodes starred George Burns and was written by Fred S. Fox and Seaman Jacobs. It was done right after George's big success in the movie *Oh God* in which he played the title role. The story was that Vera, who was quite naïve, has seen the movie and when George happens to stop by Mel's Diner, she thinks he really is God. George was in every scene and also did a song and dance with Linda Lavin. At that time he was in his late 80s, so I asked his manager Irving Fein if he would like to have cue cards. He said he'd ask him. He came back, saying, "George wants to know if any of the other actors use cue cards," and I told him no, and he said, "Then George doesn't want to use them, either." I was telling the truth because I didn't find out till much later that Vic Tayback didn't exactly use cue cards but wrote his lines on the vegetables and hamburger buns in the kitchen. Although he was a very funny guy, memorizing his speeches didn't come easily to him. On one show, he forgot and ate his own lines.

In 1981, while we were working for Warner Bros., Bob and I marked an anniversary of being a team for thirty-five years,

Christina Carroll, Bob Carroll Jr., Lucy, Madelyn, and Michael Martin at the opening of the Lucy Retrospective at the Museum of Broadcasting in New York.

and David Horowitz, head of publicity, decided that the studio should give us a party to celebrate. They could also get publicity for the two shows we were producing, *Alice* and *Private Benjamin,* and two pilots we had written for Broadway actors Dorothy Louden and David Rounds. But we didn't care what their motives were, it was a very nice gesture. We appeared with Lucy on *The Merv Griffin Show* to talk about it. The party was held on the outer court at CBS, where we got our start, now the home of KCBS-TV. The casts of both shows came, plus Lucy with her husband, Gary Morton, all our kids and many of our friends, plus some of the people who were staff writers with us long ago and guest stars of various *I Love Lucy* episodes. Eve Arden was there, also Elliott and Mary Jane Croft Lewis, Harriet Nelson with her son David, Cornel Wilde, Lloyd Bridges, Edie Adams, Barbara Eden, Jayne Meadows, and Rudy Vallee. They handed out little maps, and you could take a conducted tour of our old office on the second floor and look into Studio A, now the

Lucy appeared with Bob Carroll Jr. and Madelyn on The Merv Griffin Show *to help celebrate the 35th Anniversary of Bob and Madelyn writing together.*

newsroom, where we did the original pilot of *I Love Lucy*. There was a band, and Steve Allen acted as emcee, giving us various plaques signed by President Reagan, Governor of California Pat Brown, and John Mitchell, head of the Academy of Television Arts & Sciences. (Okay, so we were on the "send them a plaque" list for that week, but it was still terribly flattering.) It was a memorable evening and especially so since we started out as a team with Bob saying, "I'll give it a year."

In early 1986, Aaron Spelling approached Bob and me to write a series for Lucy in which she plays a grandmother, to be called called *Life With Lucy*, to be produced by Gary Morton. About this time, I also heard the news that Desi was seriously ill. I was talking to my husband Dick about Desi and remarked that I didn't think people appreciated his contribution to *I Love Lucy* and TV in general, and I hoped he knew how Bob and I felt about him. Dick suggested I write him a letter, and so I did.

March 30, 1986

Dear Desi,

As you undoubtedly know, Lucy is going to do another series. Bob and I have been asked to go along on the voyage, and of course we couldn't say no. We're not sure if it will be lots of fun or if we have lost our minds. Naturally, thinking about this project has brought back a lot of memories. It occurred to me that maybe you didn't know how many times your name comes up in our conversation and how we really feel about you. I am getting to the point in life when I think you should say something nice about someone out loud, instead of assuming they know how you feel.

Bob and I are always telling people in interviews how the whole three-camera film system was your idea and how you were the force that made *I Love Lucy* the hit it was. We have told them many times what a joy it was to work with somebody with your enthusiasm, your showmanship, and your instinctive feeling for what was good. We were so young and green then that we took this kind of thing for granted. When we got out into the real world, we realized how lucky we were to work with you, with your great gift for bringing out the best in us. What a pleasure it was to do a show with somebody who never said "That won't work" or "How much will it cost?" You always said, "Let me talk to the guys," and then you would call the prop department or special effects and outline our latest crazy scheme. I guess they thought if you thought it would work, they'd better make it work, and they did.

I was always amazed at your grasp of story, as I would tell you our latest plot idea as fast as I could in between your rehearsing a scene, and you would say,

Desi Arnaz

"I think it needs something in the second act," and you would be right. And the way you handled writers. We have tried to imitate you when we have worked on other shows, telling the writers how good their script is and how much we like it and then gradually changing half of it. And the way you also handled our favorite redhead, and the guest stars, with all your charm.

Recently, we met with Aaron Spelling for the first time to discuss the new *Lucy* show and he was so charming and complimentary to us that Bob said he must be part Cuban.

Well, I have rambled on quite a bit and, of course, I couldn't have said any of this in person. It would embarrass us both. I just thought you would like to know that a couple of writers you used to work with often think about you and fondly say your name.

Love,

Madelyn

Life With Lucy didn't work. It's easy to look back now and talk about what went wrong and why we shouldn't have done it. "You can't go home again," "lightning doesn't strike twice in the same place," and all those other clichés apply.

The premise of the show was that Lucy moved in with her daughter, son-in-law, and two small grandchildren, plus the children's other grandfather, played by the wonderfully funny Gale Gordon. Lucy loved working with Gale, but she told us she didn't want to have a running character who was a female sidekick like Vivian Vance had played for so many years. Vivian had died recently, and Lucy couldn't stand the thought of replacing her.

One of the highlights was that we had John Ritter as a guest star. Lucy had always admired him and wanted to work with him, so we wrote a show especially for him. He had several physical scenes and was hilarious. Not only was he charming and terribly funny, but he was also a real professional. He came to the set several days before the show and talked to the special effects people, and then tried to work out his stunts ahead of time. Lucy loved that because that was always the way she worked. And of course, the audience roared, and loved to see the two of them working together.

We did some pretty funny shows, and the studio audience was wildly enthusiastic, but the ratings weren't exactly sensational. *Life With Lucy* was supposed to be the kingpin of ABC's Saturday night line-up, where all the other shows were new, but it wasn't quite working out. The eleventh show we had filmed had Audrey Meadows (of *The Honeymooners* fame) as a guest star who played Lucy's sister, also named Audrey. The story line was about how Lucy's daughter had eloped and never had a fancy wedding, so on her anniversary she and her husband wanted to have a small formal wedding and repeat their vows. Lucy, who had never had a chance to be a "Mother of the Bride," was thrilled and started making plans, when her sister, Audrey, arrived for a visit. Somehow the two started clashing over just how the wedding should go. Lucy's plans got changed, and things became pretty tense. It was obvious from the start that Audrey and Lucy worked well together, with a chemistry that really clicked. Lucy, of course, recognized this, and we all immediately made plans to bring back the character of Audrey in many of the future shows. But it wasn't meant to be. After the thirteenth episode, ABC cancelled the show. Gary Morton had learned about the cancellation just before we were to film the thirteenth show, but he didn't want Lucy to hear about it before she went on, so he didn't tell anyone. The next morning I learned the news when I drove onto the lot to go to work, and the guard said "Too bad about your show being cancelled." Yes, it was.

When people learn that I wrote *I Love Lucy*, they often ask, "Did you know you were writing a classic?" Sure. Bob and I sat down and said "Okay, let's write a classic that will last more than fifty years, play in eighty countries and be seen by over a billion viewers and every hour of every day *I Love Lucy* will be playing somewhere. We told ourselves, let's write something that will become the Queen of England's favorite show, and that people like Matt Lauer on the *Today* show will use Desi's "splain" like it was part of the English language. The truth is we sat down and tried to come up with an idea for the next show.

I am still amazed when fans tell me the plots of the shows and quote the dialogue. They tell me their favorite episode and how many times they have seen it. My granddaughter, Nicole Davis, did the entire "Vitameatavegamin" routine for her school class.

But I think the greatest compliment of all is when people tell me that when they are feeling blue, they sit down, and watch an old *I Love Lucy* show, and it makes them laugh and forget about their troubles. At an *I Love Lucy* convention, when Bob and I were signing autographs, a woman made a special point of telling me that when her father was in the hospital and couldn't get well, she used to sit there every day by his bed, and the only thing that got her through it was she knew she could watch *I Love Lucy* in the afternoon. Who could ever imagine that the name of the show would be a prophecy, and everybody *would* love Lucy?

I am sitting in my office at my home and from my desk I can see all sorts of pictures. There are many of Lucy—as a clown, a candy maker, a geisha girl, a gypsy queen, an Italian grape stomper, a penguin, a kangaroo, a ballet dancer, and a seller of Vitameatavegamin. And each one reminds me of what a rare privilege I had to work with one of the world's great comedy legends. There are pictures of the *Alice* group, Eve Arden and Kaye Ballard of the *Mothers-in-Law*, Steve Allen, and all the fine actors I was fortunate to work with.

There are pictures of me with Bob, and in most of them I am laughing at something he just said. How lucky can you be to find a partner who is not only a wonderful person but who has the exact same sense of humor you do and always makes you laugh?

There are pictures of my husband Dick, my college boyfriend and my all-time serious love. This year we celebrated our forty-first wedding anniversary.

And there are lots of pictures of our children Michael Martin, Ned, Lisa, Charlotte, and Brian Davis, all of whom are intelligent, caring, charming people who I'm very proud of and who are all still speaking to us. We are very fond of our two beautiful daughters-in-law, Donna Coleman Martin and Helen Scrim Davis. And then there are our nine grandchildren: James, Ben, and Erin Schwier, and Erin's new husband Michael Stewart; Colin, Catherine and Nicole

Madelyn and Richard Davis (on couch, left) celebrate Christmas 2003 with extended family.

Davis; Matthew and Adam Sholly; and Dianna Martin, who told me I have to mention them but I was going to anyway bccausc thcy arc all so dclightful.

A few years ago, Dick and I went back to Indianapolis for my fiftieth high school reunion. In preparation, I lost five pounds and searched for just the right dress, one that looked really good but not too Hollywoodish. I remember my mother used to tell me, "Don't put on airs." I guess I thought I had something to put on airs about. Dick and I entered the party, and I was approached by a small woman I didn't recognize. She peered at my name tag and said, "Didn't you go out west and write something?"

I guess I did.

About the Authors

Madelyn Pugh Davis and her writing partner, Bob Carroll Jr., have been in the entertainment business for more than fifty years. Together they have written more than four hundred television shows—all the *I Love Lucy* shows as well as *The Lucy-Desi Comedy Hour*, *The Lucy Show*, *Here's Lucy*, *Life with Lucy*, and *The Mothers-in-Law*—and about three hundred radio shows. They have produced more than two hundred television shows.

Davis and Carroll were Executive Producers on the *Private Benjamin* and *Alice* TV series, and they also wrote for Steve Allen, Debbie Reynolds, Dorothy Loudon, and Dinah Shore.

Davis and Carroll are two-time Emmy nominees for their work on *I Love Lucy*, and they received a Golden Globe Award as the producers of *Alice*. In 2001, UCLA Film School honored Davis with a Lifetime Achievement in Television Writing.